MICHAEL H

POPE ALEXANDER VI

Renaissance Monster

2019

My books include: *Cellini* [a fully-revised 2018 edition], *Caravaggio* [a fully-revised 2018 edition], *Cesare Borgia, Renaissance Murders, TROY, Greek Homosexuality, ARGO, Alcibiades the Schoolboy, RENT BOYS, Buckingham, Homoerotic Art (in full color), Sailors and Homosexuality, The Essence of Being Gay, John (Jack) Nicholson, THE SACRED BAND, German Homosexuality, Gay Genius, SPARTA, Charles XII of Sweden, Mediterranean Homosexual Pleasure, CAPRI, Boarding School Homosexuality, American Homosexual Giants, HUSTLERS, Omnisexuality, the Death of Gay and Straight Sex* and *Christ has his John, I have my George: The History of British Homosexuality*. I live in the South of France.

CONTENTS

CHAPTER ONE

THE ORIGINS OF THE BORGIA
1416 – 1455

The Borgias' ancestors had been Spanish condottieri who had chased Muslims from Valencia, taking over a good part of their lands for themselves. Entering the university at age fourteen, the founder of the warrior segment of the Borgia, Alonso Borgia [Borja], left with two doctorates in law. Due to his expertise in canon law, he was chosen as a member of a council set up to bring an end to the Great Schism which had seen popes in both Rome and in Avignon. Rome had two families of great and competing importance, the Orsini and the Colonna, and it was a Colonna who became Pope Martin V, although there had been a holdout, an insignificant Spaniard who was proclaimed, by the vote of three cardinals, Clement VIII. Alfonso V of Aragon was the only person to recognize him.

In 1417 King Alfonso V of Aragon, a kingdom that had absorbed Alonso's birthplace of Valencia, invited Alonso to meet with him. Alfonso was just 21 and King of Sicily, Corsica and Sardinia as well as Aragon. His sights were now set on conquering Naples ever since Queen Joanna, of disputed sanity, invited him to protect the city that was under the threat of French siege. As an enticement, she decreed that he would succeed her.

At the time, Naples was a kingdom that included the whole of the south of Italy. It was a world power. It would bring Alfonso wealth and perhaps be the first building block in Alfonso's domination over the entire peninsula, from Milan to Calabria. Naples was by far the largest city, with over 100,000 people, compared to Rome's 40,000, and its origin went all the way back to the Greeks who founded Neopolis. Some Neapolitans felt they were lucky to have been chosen as the capital of the empire Alfonso envisioned, but most had seen so any dukes, lords, kings and tyrants over the centuries that they were totally indifferent now.

Alfonso had heard of Alonso Borgia and liked him enough during their first interview to make him his secretary, with the assignment of getting Martin V's accord to Alfonso's intervention in Naples. As Naples was considered to be under the jurisdiction of the church, as were the Papal States, the pope's assent was vital. Alfonso believed that Martin, tired of the feuds engendered by the Great Schism, feuds during which Spain had played a key role, would welcome him with open arms. In addition, Martin, a Colonna, was having problems as usual with the Orsini, and Alfonso felt Martin would be happy to have the virile Alfonso's backing.

The opposite occurred. Convinced by the power of France, Martin threw his support behind them. Two years of war followed, during which the French, having killed Alfonso's brother Pedro in battle, blew his body through a cannon into the Aragon lines. In retaliation

Alfonso went to Marseille and burned the city to the ground. Tired of all the fuss, Joanna went over to her former enemies and declared France her legal heir. In point of fact, Joanna was a crazy nymphomaniac who offered her kingdom to any male willing to bed her.

Alfonso and Alonso Borgia, both highly intelligent, realized that the only solution to the problem would be through very fine negotiations. Alonso was assigned to contact Martin and together they worked out a compromise. King Alfonso would drop the Spanish Clement VIII and accept Martin as the one and only legitimate pope, and Martin would recognize King Alfonso's right to Naples. Clement VIII was offered the bishopric of Palma Mallorca. In thanks for his good offices, Alonso Borgia was given the bishopric of his native Valencia, an extremely rich diocese he accepted after first taking the necessary steps to become a priest. Eventually his grandson Cesare Borgia would become Duke of Valencia.

The war for Naples continued between Aragon and France with Alfonso himself falling into the hands of Filippo Maria Visconti. Visconti was a condottiere fighting for the French and should normally have turned Alfonso over to them, but Alfonso was so charming that he ended up fascinating the sadistic tyrant, persuading him that it would be better for Milan to have the less powerful Alfonso in Naples rather than the powerful French. Alfonso was freed just when Martin died. Eugenius, the pope who replaced Martin, had discussions with Alonso Borgia whom he made a cardinal and recognized Alfonso's right to Naples. The pope also legitimized King Alfonso's bastard son Ferrante, a fairy book ending.

Eugenius was replaced by Pope Nicolas, an intelligent, honest, good man who at 49 could have been, in age, Alonso Borgia's son. He confirmed the legitimization of Ferrante. Yet he too died and was replaced--due to infighting between the Orsini and the Colonna--by the last man on earth a bookie would have put his money on, the benign Alonso Borgia himself [called Alonso de Borja at the time], now Pope Calixtus III, age 76.

Calixtus surprised everyone by ordering a crusade against the Turks, but found little following. There had been half a dozen crusades already, all of which, except the first one, had ended in disaster. A cardinal known as Scarampo was named to head the fleet the pope built with the church's money, but ships promised by Alfonso never materialized, turning Calixtus irredeemably against the man who had made him. He refused to allow King Alfonso to divorce his wife of 40 years and he refused, much more importantly for Alfonso, to ratify the bulls legitimatizing Ferrante. Young Ferrante was a sociopath, the kind only amused by the cruelest butchery. This Calixtus knew because Calixtus had been appointed Ferrante's tutor by the man he now hated, Alfonso of Aragon, Sicily, Sardinia, Corsica and Naples. But Calixtus also refused to legitimize Ferrante because he was a bastard, and a bastard son would not be allowed to reign by the moralistic Spanish, something the Italians accepted without question.

Calixtus also found help against King Alfonso in strange places. He was aided by an indomitable warrior called Skanderbeg of Albania, so invincible against the

Turks that he won Venice's favor, until he became so powerful that Venice feared the dominance of Albania over Venice and offered a reward for his head. Incredibly, Skanderbeg had been kidnapped by the Turks as a child and had worked his way up through the janissaries until switching sides. Calixtus was also helped by a character rich in color, known to us today as Dracula.

Vlad the Impaler was known by his father's name, Dracul, meaning son of the dragon. His father ruled Wallachia. He was a warrior who dedicated himself to the protection of Christians against the hordes of Ottomans of whom he is credited with impaling tens of thousands. As a boy he spoke Romanian and learned Greek, German and Latin, combat skills as well as geography, mathematics and science. Vlad and a younger brother, Radu the Handsome, were sent by their father to the Ottomans as hostages and there Radu converted to Islam. The Ottomans taught the boys warfare and horsemanship. Vlad's father was overthrown and Vlad's older brother, who should have succeeded his father, was blinded and buried alive. When Vlad eventually came to power in Wallachia he strove to increase both the defenses of the country and his own political power. He had the nobles he held responsible for his father and brother's murders impaled. When Turks arrived to reclaim tribute from Wallachia he requested that they remove their turbans in respect for his person. When they refused, he had the turbans nailed to their heads, killing them all. The Turks sent an army that Vlad defeated; the soldiers were impaled with the highest stake reserved for their general. The pope and the Venetians--whose trade had been disrupted by the Turks--were wild with joy at the news. But Radu the Handsome, who had converted to Islam, came at the head of janissary battalions to destroy his Christian brother, promising that the nobles in Wallachia who had lost their positions because of Vlad would recuperate their entire wealth. By then Vlad's reputation for evil had spread through Germany and Russia. How much is true will never be known. He was said to have had children roasted and then fed to their mothers, and to have had the breasts of women cut off and forcibly fed to their husbands, before impaling them all. Radu's army refused to cross the Danube when, in horror, they came across thousands of rotting corpses, all impaled.

Dracula.

Later we'll learn about the Sultan Mehmed II who conquered Constantinople. He was in love with Vlad's brother, Radu the Handsome, who became a janissary. When Mehmed made his intentions clear, Radu stabbed him but later ''he was the Emperor's favourite,'' wrote Patrick Balfour in his *The Ottoman Centuries*. When Mehmed ordered one of his diplomates, Notaras, to give him his 14-year-old son, the man refused. Mehmed had both decapitated and their heads placed before him at a banquet, a clear warning to others. Mehmed later was poisoned by his son who took his place.

Calixtus, so physically weak he ruled from his bed, followed up his wars with the Turks with his decision to take back the Papal States from the lords, dukes, princes and powerful families, like the Colonna and the Orsini, that ruled the countless entities comprising the States, entities that nonetheless belonged to the church situated in Rome. The States were necessary for the glory of the papacy, but also due to their importance: fertile flatlands crossed by a vital road link between Florence and the Adriatic, the Via Emilia.

For this Calixtus needed men he could count on. As there were none, he turned to boys, namely his sister's sons. One was Pier Luigi Borgia, the other was Rodrigo Borgia, Rodrigo who, when elected pope, the future Alexander VI, would continue the fight to subdue the Papal States with a boy of his own, his son Cesare. Alexander VI would soon become, along with his successor Julius II, the most powerful popes in the history of Italian Christendom.

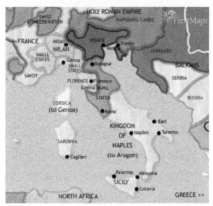

The Papal States just above the Kingdom of Naples, which held nearly two-thirds of Italy.

CHAPTER TWO

RODRIGO BORGIA'S EARLY YEARS

Rodrigo de Borja was born on the 1st of January 1431 in the town of Xativa near Valencia, in the realm of Aragon. His father was Jofrè Llançol i Escrivà and his mother Isabel de Borja y Cavanilles. Rodrigo adopted his mother's name when her uncle, Alonso de Borja became Calixtus III. [There are multiple discrepancies concerning the Borgia, concerning Pier Luigi Borgia, named as being Rodrigo's brother and his son, although two boys of the same name could well have existed, and Rodrigo's father is thought by some to have been Jofrè de Borja y Escrivà; there are also multiple disparities concerning birth and death dates.]

For the moment, Calixtus made sure the boys were educated, Rodrigo earning even a doctorate in law, the equivalent of summa-cum-laude, at Bologna. He was made cardinal at age 25 in 1456 and vice-chancellor to

Calixtus at the unheard-of age of 26. He was ordained a priest in 1468, all of the above thanks to his uncle Calixtus. He inherited the benefice of bishop of Valencia, a post he later bestowed on his son Cesare. He was also made captain-general over all papal troops--in effect Calixtus' minister of war.

Rodrigo's becoming a priest *after* becoming a cardinal is due to the fact that *anyone*, baptized and in possession of a set of balls, can become a cardinal, although the reader shouldn't hold his breath. The special chair with a hole, upon which new popes were obliged to sit while someone feels to make sure he's in possession of the authentic equipment, popularized in films, is thought by most historians to be unfounded. Celibacy came into existence during the Second Lateran Council in 1139, after which all clergy took vows of chastity.

Rodrigo would remain vice-chancellor under five popes--Calixtus, Pius II, Paul II, Sixtus IV and Innocent VIII--because he thoroughly merited the position, as he was an administrator of great competence, in addition to being cunning. As the keeper of the gate, deciding who could enter the papal apartments and who could not, he became so wealthy he could provide palaces for his mistresses, find them noble husbands, and see to the needs of his illegitimate children. Niccolò Machiavelli assistant Agostino Vespucci wrote to Machiavelli [after Rodrigo had become pope]: ''It is known to everyone that his Holiness brings 25 women or more to the Vatican each night so that the palace is made the brothel of all filth'' (2). Yet for all this, Alexander, once elected pope, never ever neglected the ruling of Rome, nor his religious duties, unlike his cardinal son, Cesare, who prided himself on his atheism and who, due to syphilis, wore more and more often a black mask, in color harmony to his black clothing, which greatly frightened the people. ''He was much irritated by the skin on his face in the lower part, which falls apart like leaves and results in a pus that he is much concerned to hide with his mask,'' wrote historian Johann Burchard (2).

A secretary, Jacopo Gherardi da Volterra, wrote ''Borgia's various offices, his numerous abbeys in Italy and Spain, and his three bishoprics of Valencia, Porto and Cartagena, yield him a vast fortune; and it is said that the office of Vice-Chancellor alone brings him in 8,000 gold florins. His plate, his pearls, his clothes embroidered with silk and gold, and his books in every department of learning are very numerous, and all are magnificent. I need not mention the innumerable-bed hangings, the trappings of his horses, the gold embroideries, the richness of his beds, his tapestries in silver and silk, nor his magnificent clothes, nor the immense amount of gold he possesses,'' a quote offered by Christopher Hibbert in his essential *The Borgia and Their Enemies*, 2008.

Calixtus' form of nepotism was accepted by the Colonna and the Orsini because it was through nepotism that they themselves had gained power and prodigious wealth. Rodrigo's brother Pier Luigi was made prefect of Rome, Duke of Spoleto and governor of Castel Sant'Angelo, a post held by the Orsini for generations. Pier Luigi ventured out from Rome to take back the tiny city-states in the environs, ruled by the Orsini, whose hatred for the pope and his nephew Rodrigo grew beyond limits. The Orsini had ruled over

Rome and its surroundings like cave-age thugs for a century. Armed, they took what they wanted when they wanted it, killing whomever they pleased, having their way with any girl that caught their fancy.

The Colonna were thrilled, naturally, with Pier Luigi's opposition to the Orsini, and informed him that he could have a Colonna bride whenever he wished. It was partially because Rodrigo performed his duties brilliantly that he was so easily accepted by the other cardinals, but in addition he is said to have been handsome and cheerful, a smooth talker but also one possessing eloquence, and people were drawn to him like ''iron is drawn to a magnet,'' wrote Veronese humanist Gaspare da Verona.

Rodrigo and his son Cesare lived and worked in tandem, like the bicycle of the same name, at times Rodrigo at the handlebars, at times Cesare. Their histories are so intertwined as to be inseparable, and even their deaths threatened to come at exactly the same moment, in exactly the same manner, and although Cesare did survive, his end soon followed, three years after the passing of his father, at age 31. That Alexander had held out until age 72 was not an accident. His instincts and intelligence were always more finely tuned than those of his son, which made him an outstanding diplomate, and the fact that they both lacked the gene of fear made their combined force awesome. Alexander's powers--and talent for self-preservation--kept him alive, while Cesare's led directly to his death.

Rodrigo was virile, producing many legitimatized children [as well as being the first pope to ever recognize his bastards] on his main mistress, Vannozza de' Catanei, two of whom become world famous, a daughter, Lucrezia, and a son, Cesare. He had at least four other children he did not recognize officially, but all his offspring and mistresses were abundantly cared for. Alexander was sensual, fun loving, certainly good to his children, a sugar-daddy papa, extremely tolerant, ruthless, courageous, and, as said, an administrator of genius. His life and that of his son Cesare will be inseparably dealt with throughout this book. Of his other children:

Very little is known about Pier Luigi Borgia, named, as stated above, Duke of Spoleto, captain general of the church, prefect of Rome and governor of Castel Sant'Angelo by Calixtus III. He was appointed 1st Duke of Gandía by his father Rodrigo. Some historians believe he was Cesare's brother, others his half-brother, meaning that he was either Rodrigo's son or Vannozza's, as she had three husbands [Dominico da Rignano, Antonio de Brescia and Giorgio di Croce], not counting a great number of other lovers, one of whom historians believe was Giuliano della Rovere, the future Julius II, Rodrigo's mortal enemy. Pier Luigi died young, having bequeathed his duchy, Gandía, the Borgia ancestral home in Spain, to this brother Juan, and 10,000 ducats to his sister Lucrezia.

It is uncertain when Juan Borgia was born, perhaps between 1474 and 1476, nor where, although Rome is likely. His mother Vannozza was married to Dominico da Rignano [also written d'Arignano], a marriage arranged by Alexander, a service he rendered all his mistresses, bringing legitimacy to them and wealth to their complacent husbands. Juan married the wife of his deceased brother Pier Luigi and fathered three children, two girls who became nuns and a son whose own son was Saint Francis Borgia [a man who became a renowned Jesuit after the death of his wife, who had given him eight children]. Juan was the 2nd Duke of Gandía, his son, another Juan, the 3rd, and the Saint the 4th. Juan's body was found in the Tiber, his throat slit and nine stab wounds to his torso, fully described in a following chapter.

Juan was admired for his svelte body and wondrous clothes, mantles of gold brocade, jewel-encrusted doublets of velvet, and his horse was recognized for the tinkling of its silver bells. The codpiece that covered his manhood was of cloth embroidered in gold or with scarlet striping, held in place by tied strings with precious pearls at the ends. The chronicler Geronimo Zurita wrote that he was spoiled, ''a mean young man, full of ideas of grandeur, haughty and cruel'', a quote from Marion Johnson's *The Borgia*, 1981. The Orsini were in continual battle with the Borgia, and when Juan came up against Carlo Orsini in 1497 Juan was ''heavily defeated in great dishonor'', wrote Burchard, a trouncing rubbed in when Orsini sent him a message of filthy content, lodged in the anus of a donkey. We know that Cesare was deeply jealous of Juan's having been chosen by his father to lead the papal troops, but Juan's feelings towards Cesare are unknown. He was certainly aware of Cesare's greater intelligence and his place as Alexander's chief advisor.

Jofrè Borgia was Alexander and Vannozza's youngest son, born in 1481 or 1482. He was wedded to Sancia of Aragon, daughter of King Alfonso II of Naples, who was forced to flee the city in advance of the troops of Charles VIII. He was 12 at the time of the marriage and sexually inoperative, while she was 16 and already carnally experienced, her known lovers Jofrè's brothers Juan and Cesare, and as she had a marked preference for older men, their father Rodrigo cannot be struck from the list of possible bedmates. The couple lived in Rome. Jofrè's relations with his father were described as distant, most probably because Rodrigo doubted that Jofrè was his son. Jofrè was suspected of having killed his brother Juan when he found out his role in pleasing his wife, a hypothesis Rodrigo couldn't accept due to the boy's docile character. It is also highly unlikely than Juan, a born warrior, would have allowed small Jofrè to get close enough to do him harm, whereas Cesare was known to have bettered Juan during the sparing combats they'd had from adolescence to adulthood.

Jofrè was given the title of Prince of Squillace and the 40,000 yearly ducats that went with it.

Sancia and Jofrè.

Lucrezia Borgia, daughter of Rodrigo and Vannozza de' Catanei, had three marriages, each politically motivated to advance the interests of the Borgia, all to be covered in detail. Like Sancia, she had innumerable sexual conquests, quasi-equivalent to those of her brothers Cesare and Juan, and has been assumed to have been incestually involved with Cesare, a scene in *Godfather* writer Mario Puzo's book *The Family* has her complaining to her father Alexander--at work at a nearby table--that his son Cesare is hurting her as he tries to enter his sister on a nearby bed. Alexander interrupts his writing to instruct his son on the proper ways of preparing a girl for painless intercourse. In the Showtime televised version of *The Borgias*, Cesare is the love of her life, and she in love with him.

Her first husband was Giovanni Sforza who was forced to accept an annulment of the marriage when Alexander found a more profitable candidate. While waiting for the annulment, Lucrezia retired to the convent of San Sisto where, in 1497, she gave birth to a boy, the father a Spanish servant. The bodies of the servant and a maiden who had secretly smuggled him into Lucrezia's apartments were found drowned in the Tiber. Two papal bulls were issued in 1501, one stating that her child, Giovanni Borgia, was Cesare's, while the second, kept secret at the time, stated he was Alexander's, seemingly proof that she was having relations with both during her marriage to Giovanni Sforza.

Her son was at her side when she married Alfonso of Aragon, the baby passed off as her half-brother. She genuinely loved Alfonso, age 17 to her 18. They had a child who died at age 12. Alphonso was murdered by Cesare, details coming.

In 1502 she married Alfonso I d'Este, an open marriage from the beginning, both sexually available to outsiders, although she did have five children with Alfonso, the paternity of which will never be known. [One of her lovers was the valiant warrior Pierre Terrail, seigneur de Bayard, known to the world as Chevalier Bayard.]

Her portrait by Bartolomeo Veneto.
A chronicler wrote that she had blonde hair that fell to the knees, a beautiful complexion, hazel eyes, a full, high bust, and natural grace that made her seem to walk on air.
She is also said to have possessed a hollow ring filled with the famous Borgia white powder ''she used frequently to poison drinks,'' a quote from *A Brief History of Poisoning*, 2013.

It was in giving birth to the tenth of her known children that she died.

CHAPTER THREE
MILAN

1447

The history of Milan that concerns us began with the Duke Filippo Maria Visconti, who reigned from

1412 to 1447, a hugely ugly and hugely fat recluse who kept to his fortress away from the sight of those--ambassadors, kings, emperors and the like--who might judge his physical hideousness. He had a dream, that of becoming lord over as much of the land surrounding Milan as militarily possible, a dream that led him to attack the Romagne, home of tiny fiefdoms such as Forlì, Imola and Faenza. He also attacked the Florence of Cosimo de' Medici. He was paranoiac to the extreme, switching bedrooms as many as three times a night to avoid assassination. He murdered his older brother Gian Maria, a ruler of incredible cruelty who dressed his dogs to devour whomever he sicced them on. During one of the wars Gian Maria waged, the people of Milan, starving to death, pleaded with him to decree peace. In response he had his soldiers massacre 200, forbidding, from then on, the word ''peace'' in Milan, under pain of death. When Filippo Maria Visconti found his wife lacking in enthusiasm to be covered by his walruse-like blubber, he accused her of having an affair with a young page and had both beheaded. He then married a girl whom he expulsed from the palace when, on the wedding night, the superstitious duke heard a dog barking--an evil omen, although on another mistress he fathered an illegitimate daughter, Bianca. Before taking any decision he had his astrologers indicate the place and time for each of his actions.

Gian Maria and Filippo Maria Visconti

The attack of Duke Filippo Maria on Florence pushed Florentine leader Cosimo de' Medici to hire a mercenary, the extraordinary Francesco Sforza. Cosimo wanted Francesco to destroy the power of Milan but Francesco Sforza hesitated before entering the city-state as he had plans to marry Bianca and take over Milan without having to wage war. His plan worked, he married the beauty, but as Duke Filippo Maria had not formally named him as his successor, Milan declared itself a republic on Duke Filippo Maria's death, a mere hiccup for Sforza who garrisoned the town and had himself declared duke. Sforza's contacts with Cosomo had been so humane and intellectually stimulating that Milan and Florence became friends. Cosimo backed Sforza financially to such an extent that Cosimo's palace became, literally, the Bank of Milan.

Venice, ever afraid of the hegemony of Milan, decided to send troops against both Florence and Milan. Florence appealed to Charles VII of France, a super power that made Venice withdraw simply by threatening to intervene. To thank Charles, Florence acknowledged France's age-old claim to Naples. Furious, Naples decided to go to war with Florence and sent troops to capture the city. Venice too decided to intervene again. Cosimo became literally sick due to the new circumstances and took to his bed. But two miracles occurred. Naples had to withdraw its army from the outskirts of Florence when France sent troops to make good on its claim to Naples, and Venice had to withdraw its troops when Constantinople fell to the Turks, the greatest threat ever to Venetian trade. For added safety, Venice united with Florence and Milan to better resist the Ottomans, and an era of peace descended over the former belligerents. To make doubly certain that peace would last, Cosimo sent the most precious of his possessions, a manuscript by Livy, to Ferrante, King of Naples--itself now safe thanks to the timely death of Charles VII. Although a psychopath, Ferrante loved ancient learning and, overjoyed, he promised eternal peace between Naples and Florence.

So here we have the powers that will concern this story as it unfolds: Milan, Florence, France, Venice and Naples. Rome, too, remained without papal authority, a land where livestock grazed on terrain surrounded by the crumbling marble columns of what had once been Imperial Rome, and would remain so until the advent of Alexander VI--the first and, with his son Cesare, the greatest of the Borgia, followed by Julius II, the Warrior Pope (1). With the death of Cosimo de' Medici, succeeded by his son Piero, all hell would break out.

In Milan Francesco Sforza died and was replaced by his son Galeazzo Maria Sforza, age twenty-two. Galeazzo had been trained in combat by his father and was therefore feared. When the Duke of Ferrara decided, along with Venice, to take advantage of Cosimo's son Piero's weakness as a leader by invading Florentine territory, Galeazzo sent 1,500 troops to Florence's aid. The Duke of Ferrara discovered that, although the citizens of Florence were unsatisfied with Piero, they would not rise up against him, as the duke had been led to believe. So he retraced his steps and returned to Ferrara. The Doge of Venice continued on, however, forcing Piero to seek help from not only Naples and Milan, but also from a very feared condottiere, Federico da Montefeltro of Urbino, a city-state on the edge of the Romagna.

They all came together in the main square of Florence, the Piazza della Signoria, where Lorenzo de' Medici rode up with 3,000 soldiers the Florentines had assembled, the very young Lorenzo splendid in his full armor. Galeazzo withdrew his forces for reasons he never explained, and so it was that Lorenzo's troops, and those of Federico da Montefeltro, clashed with a Venetian army led by Bartolmeo Colleoni. The battle ended indecisively even though both sides claimed victory.

Federico da Montefeltro.

By far the most impressive condottiere of the period was Federico da Montefeltro. He was a Renaissance man, the possessor of a truly wonderful bureau done in *trompe-l'oeil*. He's thought to have killed his stepbrother Oddantonio, made easy by the people of Urbino who were unhappy with his reign. Montefeltro inspired loyalty among his men, sharing his gains as condottiere with them, and because his fees were high, he was able to enrich Urbino. He had surgeons remove part of his nose so that he could see in all directions with the eye remaining him, the other having been lost in a tournament. He fought for Florence, for Milan, for Naples, and then against Florence before the Treaty of Lodi brought peace to the three city-states. The Treaty ended quarrels concerning the boundaries between the belligerents and confirmed the position of each duke, prince, count or doge as the head of his particular city-state. After the death of Francesco Sforza, Montefeltro assisted Francesco's son Galeazzo Maria Sforza in governing Milan.

At the death of Piero, Lorenzo was asked by the city nobility to take his place, which he did at age twenty, bowing modestly before the aged men standing before him. His first guest to his palace was Galeazzo Maria Sforza, accompanied by his soon-to-be-famous daughter, Caterina. Unknown to the nobles who requested his leadership, Lorenzo, fearing that he would be brushed aside as being too young and inexperienced, had sent messages to Galeazzo requesting troops, should he be forced to take power through arms. Galeazzo answered by putting a thousand men on the road to Florence. To thank him, Lorenzo put at Galeazzo's disposal every culinary, artistic and erotic pleasure at his disposal. Galeazzo returned to Milan decided to rebuild the city and stock it with art along the lines of Florence. But Galeazzo was becoming less sane each day and, luckily for all, he was soon assassinated.

Galeazzo Maria Sforza.
Galeazzo Maria Sforza, Duke of Milan, was thought to be a psychopath who didn't hesitate to tear

off a man's limbs with his own hands or rape a woman, noble or not. His sexual appetite was hard to appease but once his lust fulfilled, the woman was handed to his entourage for their needs. He detested poachers, strangling one to death on a rabbit pushed down his throat and another was nailed inside a coffin and then buried alive. A priest who predicted Galeazzo would have a short life was starved to death. Galeazzo was finally brought down by three conspirators, one of whom was a very young man named Girolamo Olgiati who, thanks to Galeazzo's library to which the duke gave him access, was able to read the lives of Brutus and Cassius and how they tried to bring republicanism back to Rome through the assassination of Caesar, a perfect example of how the ancient texts formed the Renaissance mind, Olgiati's ideal for Milan. A second conspirator, known only as Lampugnano, had obscure motives concerning land deals. The third conspirator was Carlo Visconti whose sister had been dishonored by the duke, a motive of importance today but at the time everyone was throwing his daughter or wife at Galeazzo in hopes of gaining profit. They met in church. Who struck first is in question, but the version I prefer has Visconti [the boy whose sister had been raped] on his knees as if requesting a favor as the duke walked down the nave. When Galeazzo paused to listen to him, Visconti plunged his dagger into the duke's genitals. The other men followed suit. Galeazzo, at age 32, was dead before he hit the marble flooring. The three assassins, certain of public support, did not bother to hide. Instead of thanking them, the citizens of Milan killed Lampugnano instantly and then dragged his body through the streets; the other two were caught later by Galeazzo's guard and were disemboweled, quartered and decapitated. As he was dying one of the three is reported to have shouted out, ''Death is perhaps terrible, but honor and glory are eternal!'' Which may be true as I'm retelling the story *500 years* after the event.

CHAPTER FOUR

CALIXTUS

1455

When King Alfonso of Aragon died, a man of great intelligence, a ruler of vision, Calixtus cried out, ''At last free!'' As Ferrante hadn't been legitimized, Calixtus simply issued a bull bringing Naples back into the Holy See.

The city Calixtus now reigned over, Rome, had around 40,000 inhabitants [compared to Naples that had 100,000]. The Vatican was old and crumbling after a thousand years of wear, and the city itself was a stink hole where the Forum, that had seen Triumphs of unimaginable splendor, was now a field of weeds fit only for feeding livestock. ''The dead of night covered all things,'' wrote humanist Egidio of Viterbo. ''Besides domestic tragedies, never were sedition and bloodshed more widespread; never were bandits more numerous, never more wickedness in the city; never were informers and assassins more used. Men were safe neither in their rooms, nor their houses, nor their castles. The laws of God and man were as nothing. Gold, violence and lust ruled undisputed'' (7).

''Slavery, which had almost disappeared from Italy, had returned: twenty thousand men, women and children passed through the slave market in Venice alone each year. So plentiful was the supply than even small merchants could buy a human animal to help out in the home while the nobility came more and more to rely upon them in place of expensive and arrogant servants. Prices varied immensely so that the lady of the house could expect to pay only six ducats for a hard-working but ill-favored woman while the pretty young girl who would probably grace her husband's bed would cost anything up to a hundred. The purchaser had the choice of a half-dozen races, white as well as black, Christian as well as pagan or Moslem. 'Tartars are hardiest and best for work. Russians are built on finer lines but, in my opinion, Tartars are best. Circassians are a superior breed wherefore everybody seeks them,' a Roman lady noted. They were, on the whole, well treated. In some cities, notably Florence, the children of slaves automatically became free citizens. Romans declined such an expensive sop to conscience but a slave in a household such as Cardinal Borgia's could expect a life far more attractive than that of the average peasant farmer'' (4).

During the conclave that elected Calixtus the cardinals had been shut in behind closed doors and windows, the air fetid, the exchanges of who-gets-what-for-their-vote taking place in the only partially private room, the basilica latrines, used less and less for relief because the cardinals were given less and less to eat, an encouragement to a conclusion, since conclaves had been known to go on for months in order for one man to obtain 2/3^{rds} of the votes required. The Papal College *always* consisted of Orsini and Colonna from Rome, Sforza from Milan, Medici from Florence, Este from Ferrara and at least one Gonzaga from Mantua. Calixtus had his work cut out for him, as the last one, Nicholas V, had been honest and had honestly enriched the Vatican treasury, as well as doing what he could to shore up decaying Rome and the basilica that he had recently reinforced with 2,500 cartloads of stones taken from the Colosseum (3). Nicholas had brought peace to Rome, but outside its walls city-states had been at each other's throats since the fall of the Roman Empire, the major players Venice, Milan, Florence and Bologna, while Rome not only remained neutral, but Nicholas succeeded, at the end of his pontificate, to form the Most Holy League, which brought momentary peace among the belligerents. Worse still was taking place outside of Italy, in Constantinople, where, in 1453, 21-year-old Mehmed II attacked the city, its inhabitants, 50,000, raped, butchered or sold into slavery.

Once elected, Calixtus declared war on the Turks, which meant, in part, fighting against one's own, for the youths captured in Constantinople, and thousands of boys rounded up in raids throughout Europe, formed the strongest segment of Mehmed's janissaries, youths beautifully clothed, none of whom ever went hungry, trained to be elite soldiers, to capture young replacements and women for their loins and the slave market, boys who found companionship among their own, who paired for sexual relief, and were honored when the sultan granted access to his bed. On the battlefield, European soldiers and Muslim soldiers could often speak to each other across their lines, the Muslim boys remembering the languages they had spoken before capture, yet were now converted Muslims to the death. It was Mehmed who started the tradition of strangling one's brothers on ascension to the throne, while pregnant girls in the harem were drowned like cats, a thorough disposal that Machiavelli would have found perfectly justifiable, if a new leader wished to survive.

Mehmed, by the way, had a son, Cem, who was forced to flee the Ottoman Empire because he was threatened by his brother Bayezid II [who would later poison his father Mehmed II and take the throne]. He took shelter with Innocent VIII and was later protected by Rodrigo, then Alexander VI. He was given over to Charles VIII who planned to set him up in Constantinople, which Charles aimed to capture. But Cem suddenly died, a very long segment of which is covered in the wondrously beautiful Showtime production *The Borgias*, in which the Borgia are responsible for his poisoning. In the series Cem's an extremely handsome boy, physically involved with Lucrezia. In reality, he was with Charles, miles away from the Borgia when he died, and he probably died of overeating, because he was as fat as a walrus, certainly not material for Lucrezia.

The crusade to retake Jerusalem was the aim of Calixtus' life, and he had the treasure left by Nicholas to see it through. But his efforts came too late. Europe had lost interest in crusades, bottomless wells in money and men. He did manage to send off a fleet five months after his election, headed by Pietro Urrea, a bishop, chosen because he was a Spaniard, but one not in the vein of Cortés and Pizarro. Once in charge, Urrea turned to piracy, his victims the Christian ships he looted.

Another of Calixtus' problems was the Malatesta, the word meaning evil-heads, lords centered around Rimini, that I would like to introduce here: The Malatesta were a family of hotheads, schemers and murderers who ruled Rimini from 1295 until the arrival of Cesare Borgia who extinguished them with the ease of blowing out a candle. The first Malatesta was a hunchback, Giovanni [ca. 1240 – 1304], called Giovanni the Lame, who killed his wife Francesca and his brother Paolo when he discovered them *in flagrante delicto*:

Francesca and Paolo by Ingres.

Paolo was called *"Il Bello"* and the affaire had been going on for ten years. The great writer Boccaccio claims that Francesca's father favored her marriage to Giovanni as a way of promoting good relations between his family and the Malatesta, but fearing that Francesca would refuse a cripple, he had her believe that she would be wedding the far more handsome Paolo. It was only following the wedding night, after she had surrendered her virginity to the boy she loved, that she discovered the ruse. A perfect story *à la Boccaccio*.

The murdered Paolo had a son, Ramberto. He was contacted by a cousin, Uberto, who wanted to kill Pandolfo I Malatesta, Lord of Rimini, and take his lands. But Uberto was the son of Giovanni Malatesta, Giovanni the Lame, the murderer of Ramberto's father. In the finest Italian tradition of treachery, Ramberto invited Uberto to a banquet to finalize plans for the murder, but it was Uberto himself the main course.

Ramberto then planned to gain total power over the lands of his cousins by eliminating two other Malastesta, Malatesta II Malatesta and Ferrantino Malatesta. As a banquet had worked so well the first time, he organized a second, inviting both cousins. Ferrantino showed up but Malatesta II Malatesta couldn't make it. Ferrantino was made prisoner, escaping death until Malatesta II could be imprisoned too. But Malatesta II came with an army. He freed Ferrantino and forced Ramberto to flee.

Ferrantino's son, Malatesta Novello, understood what no other member of the family seems to have been able to comprehend, that Ramberto and his plots and intrigues would only stop with the death of Ramberto himself. So Malatesta Novello invited Ramberto to his own banquet where he plunged a knife into Ramberto's neck, but not before giving his uncle time to beg for his precious life. Ramberto was said to have been dead before his body hit the marble floor.

Sigismondo Pandolfo Malatesta [1417 – 1468] was called the Wolf of Rimini. A fearless condottiere, he was also a poet and patron of the arts. He began his conquests at age 13 against Carlo II Malatesta who wanted to annex Rimini. He took over Carlo's lands and became lord of Rimini at age 15. He later gained Pesaro by defeating his own brother Malatesta Novello. He married Ginevra d'Este but had her poisoned when a better match offered itself, that with Polissena Sforza. He fought for the pope and then against him, for Naples and then against it, for the Sforza and then against them, this last treason ending in the death of his wife Polissena whom he had ordered his servants to drown like a cat.

He had a number of sons from a huge variety of mistresses, one of whom was beheaded by her husband, Rodolfo Gonzaga, when he found out. Sigismondo's third wife was Isotta degli Atti, his long-time mistress. He was accused by Pope Pius II of incest with one of his sons, Roberto. The pope sent a fifteen-year-old priest, the Bishop of Fano, to notify him of his excommunication for incest and a number of treasons. He publicly sodomized the boy in the square of Rimini, in front of his applauding troops. Sodomy was such a Renaissance pastime that the Germans called it *Florenzer*, anal sex *à la Florentine*

In Rome a procedure called the canonization into Hell was brought against Sigismondo. In an unprecedented ceremony--not repeated since--he was sent to Hell and its eternal flames. His image was burned in public and war was declared against him by a league encompassing the pope, the King of Naples and the Dukes of Milan and Montefeltro. He defeated them all except for Federico da Montefeltro, the greatest condottiere to have perhaps ever lived, who took all his land, which he later returned to the pope and the Papal States, leaving Sigismondo only Rimini.

In an understatement, the historian Francesco Guicciardini described Sigismondo as an enemy of ''the peace and peace lovers,'' a man who lived for intrigue and duplicitous dealings, in that sense a veritable Renaissance Italian, coupled with the fact that sexually he went from men to women and back with total abandon. He attempted to justify the ''disorders'' in his life in sonnets to his third wife, Isotta.

He ended as a highly respected condottiere under Venice. Rimi went to his son Sallustio after his death, but was recuperated by the son he had sodomized, Roberto.

Francesco Guicciardini was a major Italian historian, his masterpiece *The History of Italy.* ''No man is more disgusted than I with the ambition, avarice and profligacy of priests, not only because these vices are hateful in themselves, but also because they are utterly repugnant in those who claim to have a special relation with God. Nonetheless, my position at the Court of several popes forced me to desire their greatness for the sake of my own interest." (7)

Roberto, the victim of his father Sigismondo's incest, was a fearless condottiere, smart enough to align himself with the great Federico da Montefeltro and win back Rimini from his father's designated heir, Sallustio, son of Sigismondo's beloved mistress and then wife Isotta. He made peace with Isotta and his two half-brothers, Sallustio and Valerio, and, in the Malatesta family tradition, threw a banquet for them all, during which they were poisoned. Years later Machiavelli in his *The Prince* would write that this was the only possible way for a ruler to deal with his competition, that his choice was between the extinction of potential rivals or his own extinction later one.

As said, in 1475 Pope Sixtus IV confirmed him as Lord of Rimini and, more importantly, Federico da Montefeltro--who possessed the real power in the region--gave him his daughter. Once this was all accomplished Roberto up and died of malaria. His son Pandolfo took his place until forced to flee Rimini before the troops of Cesare Borgia, thusly ending the line of the Malatesta.

The sweltering summer months of July and August provoked fevers that carried off nearly every pope unable to escape to highland retreats. With Calixtus too ill to move to the mountains, certain to die, the Orsini took to the streets crying vengeance against all Spaniards, many of whom were killed. Rodrigo, bravely, remained next to Calixtus until he rendered his last breath. Rodrigo would be courageous throughout his entire life, no matter the later heinous acts he would be accused of, a fearlessness his son Cesare inherited in its entirety.

Cesare Borgia.

''This lord,'' wrote Machiavelli, ''is very splendid and magnificent, and there is no warlike enterprise so great that it does not seem small to him. In pursuit of land and glory he knows neither fatigue nor danger. He arrives in one place before men know he has left another. He is liked by his soldiers and has collected the best men in Italy; for this reason he is victorious and formidable, and has added to that perpetual good fortune.'' (7)

CHAPTER FIVE

RODRIGO BORGIA BECOMES POPE ALEXANDER VI

The conclave to choose the next pope was set in motion. The Vatican was walled off. The clear winner was thought to be Cardinal d'Estouteville of France, cousin to the King of France and immensely wealthy. On the first vote he received only his own ballot, proof of the maxim: He who enters the conclave pope, leaves a cardinal.

What took place next was pure drama, knowledge of which has come down to us in a document written by the cardinal of Siena, the only time in the history of the church that the contents of a conclave have been divulged. We're told that d'Estouteville offered a part of his fortune to all the cardinals, telling them that the first vote was a fluke, and that he was now but one ballot short of winning. In the secrecy of the latrines, the only private place to talk, as stated earlier, he promised something to everyone, promising Rodrigo that he would continue as vice-chancellor. The cardinal of Siena tells us that he [the cardinal of Siena] was so offended by d'Estouteville's latrine shit that he mounted a counter-offensive. He met with Rodrigo, calling him a ''boy'' and a ''fool'' for believing d'Estouteville, assuring him that not only would a Frenchman be the next vice-chancellor, but also that the papacy would be moved back to French Avignon.

In the election the next day the cardinal of Siena was three votes short of winning. The cardinals decided to meet together in silence until one or several broke it by publically changing his secret vote for oral support. The first to do so was Rodrigo himself, who declared for the cardinal of Siena. This was followed by another cardinal. Colonna, seeing that the cardinal of Siena was certain to win and wanting to cast the critical vote that would swing the election and assure Colonna of the new pope's gratitude, rose to do the same. He was halted by d'Estouteville who tried to drag him out of the room. Colonna nonetheless had time to shout out ''I accede to Piccolomini,'' making the cardinal of Siena the new pope, Pius II.

G.J. Meyer, in his wonderful *The Borgia*, informs us that Rodrigo had admitted to Pius II that he was going to vote for d'Estouteville for reasons entirely of self-interest. Such candor, says Meyer, ''will be characteristic of Rodrigo over the next forty-five years, helping to explain his almost uncanny ability to win the affection of almost anyone who came within his reach.'' Pius reaffirmed Rodrigo in his function as vice-chancellor, calling him ''an extraordinarily able man'', and took a fatherly interest in the boy, finding in the already fat Rodrigo someone totally open to Pius' teaching.

Pius was one of 18 children, dirt poor, who studied law. His friends reportedly broke up with laughter when he announced that he was to become a monk because his joy in the delights of the flesh had already made him the father of several bastards. He walked with a limp caused by a pilgrimage to a shrine of the Virgin, over ice and through snow.

Rodrigo's brother Pier Luigi, in open dispute with the Orsini, was convinced to return to Spain for his own safety and Pius named a Colonna as prefect of Rome, his reward for the Colonna vote. A Pius nephew took over Rodrigo's role as head of the papal army. Readers of Robert Caro's monumental life of Lyndon Johnson will recognize a trait Rodrigo and Johnson had in common: both took every position they fought tooth and nail to acquire not only with fanatical seriousness, but developed it into something colossal, milking it for all it was worth. Johnson worked tirelessly to become president, Rodrigo did the same to become pope. Michelangelo had said of himself, ''I work harder than any man who has ever lived,'' and it was true, a truth that could have been applied to Rodrigo Borgia.

Because of continued problems with the Turks, Pius ended disputes with Naples by declaring Ferrante its new ruler. He then tried to mount a crusade against the Turks but failed when France, whose claim over Naples had been disregarded by Pius, and Venice, who sought peace with the Turks through negotiation, refused to take part. In world history no enterprise suffered more defeats and ended up killing more people--and was a bottomless pit for more money--than the crusades. Christians against Moslems; Christians against Christians, which led even to the sacking of Constantinople by Christians; inhumanity the likes of which have rarely been seen on the face of the earth; acts of horror that have blackened the reputations of kings, like Richard Coeur de Lion, and blackened Christianity itself. Calixtus had failed; and now Pius II would fail too. He would make it to Ancona where he planned to see the crusade he financed set off, only to die, of fever, perhaps bubonic. Rodrigo would be stricken too and his doctors were certain that he too wouldn't survive. His illness came as a surprise because on the ride from Rome to Ancona Rodrigo had organized banquets and the accompanying orgies.

But for the moment Pius had left Rome to take the waters in Tuscany, from where he wrote an extraordinary letter to Rodrigo who was in Siena, stating that Rodrigo had become the laughing stock of Italy owing to his participation in debauchery, an example of the pot calling the kettle black, given Pius' own lust and his own sowing of oats when he was Rodrigo's age.

''We have learned that three days ago a large number of women of Siena, adorned with all worldly vanity, assembled in the garden of Giovanni di Bichio, and that your Eminence, in contempt of the dignity of your position, remained with them from one o'clock until six and that you were accompanied by another cardinal. We are told that ... you yourself behaved as though you were one of the most vulgar young men of the age. I should blush to record all that I have been told'' (2).

Rodrigo played next to no part of the conclave of 1464 because he was suffering from the aftermath of the Alcona plague. Cardinal Pietro Barbo of Venice was elected, taking the name of Paul II, although originally he had chosen Pope Formosus, meaning beautiful, but had been talked out of it. Son of Eugenius IV through an incestuous coupling with his sister, passed off as Eugenius' nephew, he was made a cardinal at age 23. Meyer says he was ''tall and handsome ... lived simply and kept himself free of scandal.'' Most other sources maintain that he spent his life in the company of male prostitutes, that he himself, when pope, organized a carnival that was a nonstop orgy, and that he suffered a heart attack at age 54 while being butt-fucked by his lover, said some, by a favored page claimed others.

1471

Paul II kept Rodrigo as vice-chancellor, as did his successor Sixtus IV. Sixtus was the son of a poor fisherman whose title to glory was built on undreamed of nepotism, bringing to Rome a family of fishmongers and appointing, over the papal troops, a boy who had literally been selling apples on the streets of Liguria when he learned of his uncle's election. Scurrying to Rome, the boy quickly rose through the ranks, humping prepubescent girls and marrying into the Sforza of Milan, forcing the hymen of his Sforza bride, Caterina, age 10, with the full consent of Caterina's father whom she adored and who *knew* what was awaiting her (1). In point of fact, Sixtus' family was an early version of Ettore Scola's *The Down and Dirty [Brutti, sporchi et cattivi]*. Sixtus' only success, as far as his family was concerned, was his raising his nephew, the handsome Giuliano della Rovere, to the dignity of cardinal, at age 18, the future Julius II, arguably the church's most powerful pope ever [Alexander VI weighing in a close second] (8).

Sixtus doted on his family because the family, detecting his intellectual gifts, had pooled their resources to assure the dirt-poor Sixtus' education. Sixtus loved one nephew so much that he was believed to have been both Sixtus' son and his lover, as Sixtus adored boys, one of the reasons for bringing his nephews to Rome [an accusation made against Sixtus and Giuliano della Rovere, mentioned earlier]. They were louts, yes, but beautiful louts. His son-cum-lover was Pietro Riario. Sixtus turned over bishoprics to the young sire, making him fabulously rich although not enough to cover the boy's debauches, his horse racing, his deprivation. Pietro was a Renaissance man in that he gave himself to both men and women. He was on the most intimate terms with the murderous Galeazzo Maria Sforza of Milan, both eating from the same plate and sleeping in the same bed. The untoward career of the young Pietro ended at age 28--some say due to a fever, others due to indigestion because the boy adored huge banquets, and still others the usual poison--to the incommensurable chagrin of his father/lover Sixtus. Because the pope only trusted his family, the young Pietro was replaced by Girolamo, the lummox who ruptured his wife's hymen at age 10, and named him head of the papal troops. Sixtus did, however, improve Rome by widening the streets and encouraging the construction of new palaces, by restoring ''the Cloaca Maxima and its complex sewage system'' (4), and by bringing in artists and founding the Sistine Chapel Choir, filling it with beautiful lads.

1472

Rodrigo extended his palace and enriched its furnishings and his clothes. Sixtus awarded him with bishoprics and abbeys, sources of more wealth still.

Sixtus sent Rodrigo to Spain where the marriage between Ferdinand and Isabella was in dispute. At age six Isabella had been promised to Ferdinand but later, when it was suggested that she marry Edward IV of

England or his brother the future Richard III, killer of infants, she held strong to her desire to wed Ferdinand. An obstacle to their union was their consanguinity. To overcome her brother's disapproval she was forced to escape to the wedding site, Valladolid, where she was joined by and married to Ferdinand, who had been disguised as a servant to avoid the king's army. Rodrigo found a solution: ''In Spain he displayed his intelligence, tact, discretion, good humour, and confidence to do what was necessary to regularize the marriage'' (2). When the king died she was crowned, but for the first years she had to wage war against those who thought they had a better claim to the throne than she. Even Portugal invaded in an attempt to seize power. Her place finally became legitimized with the birth of a son.

In Spain Rodrigo had visited his native Valencia, his episcopal seat, where he was so wonderfully received that he remained in Spain for 14 months. On his way back his ship was wrecked off the coast of Tuscany and he was taken to Pisa to recover from his close call with death. There, at a banquet in his honor, he met Vannozza de' Catanei, the mother of his future children. In very quick succession she gave him Pier Luigi, Cesare, Juan, Lucrezia and Jofrè. In return, Rodrigo gave Vannozza a series of complaisant husbands and great wealth. These children were, however, only part of the brood he fathered with other acquaintances. The incredible luck of the Borgia was in having so many children, so many boys, boys who survived infancy in times when at least half of all children died nearly immediately or within a few years of birth. The death toll was so high that even in France, nearly up to modern times, children were given out to wet nurses who cared for them until around age seven; in this way parents suffered less when babies they'd rarely seen passed away. She had another boy, Ottaviano, which was probably not Rodrigo's, since around the time of his birth she had already had a total of three husbands.

''In later years, the charge was to be made that Vannozza Catanei came from the class of courtesan. The few certain facts about her origin indicate that her family was probably from the lowest ranks of the nobility. She was ineradicably middle-class in her approach to life. The dominant characteristics of the courtesan were generosity and improvidence. Few died wealthy, most died in utter want, justifying the belief and hope of the respectable that 'Venus reduces her worshipers to her own nudity' '' (4).

When Cesare was eight, Rodrigo moved all of his children to the home of his Spanish cousin Adriana da Mila, more qualified to raise them as she was of noble birth and would instruct them in the ways of the aristocracy. Adriana had married into the very powerful Orsini family. Her son married a beautiful girl known as La Bella whom Rodrigo immediately took as his mistress.

The next pope, Innocent VIII, was known as the Rabbit for his lack of authority. Because Sixtus had depleted the wealth so carefully amassed by Nicholas V, the new pope was forced to sell offices to the highest bidder, money spent in part on his mistresses and illegitimate children. Bands of youths, armed with daggers and swords, ruled the streets of Rome, stealing, raping and murdering to such an extent that the cardinals were forced to place guards with crossbows and artillery at their windows and on the roofs of their palaces. He fell ill and was obliged to drink the milk of nursing mothers. At his death, the cardinals who met in conclave were decided on replacing him with a strong pope who would bring order to Rome.

1492

Following the usual bargaining, during which wagonloads of gold, silver, jewels and precious furnishings and tissues were loaded at the Borgia palace and unloaded at the residences of nearly all of the cardinals [a few were said to have refused the bribes], Rodrigo Borgia became Pope Alexander VI. The truth of the bribes will never be known, and anyway, those who ran against him for pope were at least equally wealthy and equally inclined to bribe whomever they could. ''Now we are in the power of a wolf, the most rapacious perhaps that his world has ever seen. And if we do not flee, he will inevitably devour us all,'' remarked Giovanni di Lorenzo de' Medici (2). Not all agreed: ''At the news of Alexander's election to the papacy, the city of Rome went into rejoicing. One onlooker noted, 'Mark Anthony himself was not received so magnificently by Cleopatra'. Nor was the applause merely local: 'Everywhere and especially in Rome, people were seized with a lively emotion, as if God had chosen this prince as the instrument of His special designs,'' a quote from Gerard Noel's *Renaissance Popes*. Alexander now had rule over lands stretching, on the west, from Civitavecchia and Rome to, on the east, Alcona and the lands of the Malastesta, centered around Rimini on the Adriatic, the wealth from which assured him a yearly income of 100,000 florins (2).

Also in 1492 Lorenzo *Il Magnifico* de' Medici died. The contrast between the arrival of absolute evil, in the form of Alexander VI, and the exit of absolutely good, was stunning.

As mentioned, Alexander had a new mistress, Giulia Farnese, known as La Bella. Giulia had married Andrea da Mila Orsini's son, Orsino Orsini [Adriana da Mila was the woman Alexander had chosen to bring up his children as aristocrats]. Giulia had a brother, Alessandro Farnese, that Alexander now made cardinal at the same time as Cesare, causing great unrest among the cardinals who knew about his liaison with Adriana da Mila Orsini and La Bella. This was the first step in the rise of the House of Farnese, as Alessandro would later become the homosexual Paul III (10). Rodrigo was omnisexual, although he leaned towards the heterosexual side. He refused La Bella permission to visit her husband, whom Rodrigo had banned to the country. She nonetheless insisted on seeing him, preferring perhaps his beauty and youth to Rodrigo's, the cardinal age 59 to her 17, a difference of 42 years, and he had always been described as fat. He ordered her back to him, writing this letter: ''We know the evil of your soul and of the man who guides you [her husband] but we would never have thought it possible for you to break your solemn oath not to go near

Orsino. But you have done so to give yourself once more to that stallion. We order you, under pain of eternal damnation, never again to go" (2). She had no choice, as her husband, in fear of losing his life, told her to return to Rodrigo.

Despite his age and girth, the pope's virility seems to have been intact, for his interest in girls of slender waist was said to have been insatiable. At the same time, it must be said that he was just as insatiable and voracious in his appetite for work.

Alexander and his children spoke Spanish when together, but they all knew Italian, French and Latin. Cesare was destined for the orders, a destiny he hated as he hated his brother Juan who was marked for a military career, one Juan loved but was not good at--or at least not as good as Cesare would show himself to be. Cesare was ambitious to the extreme and fearless--in fact, fearing nothing and no one. Cesare addressed Juan as his Lord brother, and admonished him to give thanks to their father His Holiness, who had made the family so great.

1493

Early in the year, Cesare wrote a letter to his brother Juan, which illustrates with what respect he held his father Alexander and Juan himself, whom Cesare would murder four years later: ''We have reason, my Lord brother, to kiss the ground on which His Holiness walks and to pray always for the life of him who has made us so great; and therefore I pray you to seek continually to serve and please His

Holiness, in a manner that you may show him on our behalf our gratitude in every way that we can" (2). Juan was 19 years old, Cesare 18.

Cesare Borgia.
The Ferrarese ambassador wrote that he had great personal charm, carried himself like a prince, was lively, merry and fond of society, strong-spirited, strong-willed and fearless (3). It is known that he liked racing horses, bullfighting and carnal unions, and that he disliked wearing his ecclesiastical clothing.

While Cesare was seeking ways to please Alexander, the College of Cardinals had had enough of his tyrannical ways, their opposition so strong that Alexander responded in an audacious and stunning way. He added 13 new popes to the College, among them his son Cesare, age 18, and, as reported, the son of one of his mistresses, Alessandro Farnese. The outraged cardinals were led by Alexander's mortal enemy, Giuliano della Rovere, the future Julius II, but the fear of Alexander was such that 4 abstained, 7 approved, and 10 voted against, 11 to 10. On the 23rd of

September 1493 Alexander placed the red hat on his son's bowed head, the father flushed with pride, the son smoldering, now obliged to wear robes when what he wanted most in the world was to wear armor. He was perhaps even then plotting in his mind to kill Juan who, as the first born, was marked for military service, the second son service to the church, which, in reality, was simply Alexander's way of raising Cesare to eventually replace him--over the Romagna at the very least, perhaps over the Romagna and Naples [*the southern half of Italy*], and, with great luck, over all of a united Italy.

But Giuliano della Rovere would always be there to stand in the way, about whom a Venetian envoy reported: ''No one has any influence over him, and he consults few or none. It is always impossible to describe how strong and violent and difficult he is to manage. In body and soul he has the nature of a giant. Everything about him is on a magnified scale, both his undertakings and his passions. He inspires fear rather than hatred, for there is nothing in him that is small or meanly selfish'', a quote from John Norwich's *Absolute Monarchs*, 2011.

CHAPTER SIX

THE FIRST ITALIAN WAR

THE INVASTION OF CHARLES VIII

1494

1494 was one of the most eventful years in Alexander's life. Because he considered Naples under papal authority, as did his uncle Calixtus, he gave parts to his sons Cesare and Juan. King Ferrante of Naples naturally objected. He had the backing of Florence, Milan and Venice, and sought that of Spain. Spain hesitated because it was negotiating the division of the world into spheres, the result of which would place the New World in Spain's lap, with its mindboggling wealth [wealth that hadn't as yet been discovered]. The result of the negotiations was the Treaty of Tordesillas, of truly immense importance to the voyages of discovery that would take place afterwards.

It's surprising that the Portuguese allowed Alexander the role of arbitrator when the world was divided into two spheres, the Spanish allowed authority over one half, the Portuguese possession of the other, due to Alexander being of Spanish origin. What also made the treaty extraordinary is that both sides would respect it. The Americas went to Spain, although the line did cut through the bulge in South America, giving Brazil to Portugal. Later, with the rise of Protestantism, England and the Netherlands refused to recognize a division of the world brokered by a Catholic pope, as did France for political reasons.

The line of demarcation did not encircle the Earth. Spain and Portugal could conquer new lands they were the first to discover, although, basically, the west belonged to Spain, the east to Portugal. Discord arose, as when cloves were found, worth their weight in gold, but here too a surprising number disputes were settled through treaties, any loss compensated for in coin.

The Treaty of Tordesillas ended when François I declared, ''Show me Adam's will.''

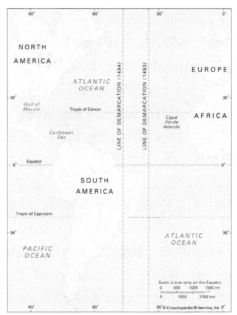

The Treaty of Tordesillas, the line to the right 1493, the line to the left 1494.

In gratitude, Spain helped Alexander and Naples find a way to peace, which Alexander sealed by giving his son Jofrè to Ferrante's son's daughter Sancia.

At the death of Ferrante that year, his son Alfonso II succeeded him. Charles VIII decided the time had come to claim certain rights France had over Naples. In this he was joined by Ludovico *Il Moro* Sforza, Duke of Milan.

Ferrante had never appreciated Alexander, and it was he who gave this picture of the pope: ''The Pope has no respect for the Holy Chair and leads such a life that people turn away in horror. By fair means or foul, he seeks nothing but the aggrandizement of his children. What he wants is war, and has persecuted me without cease since the first day of his pontificate. There are more soldiers than priests in Rome. The Pope desires war and rapine" (11).

Lorenzo de' Medici died relatively young from complications probably due to family gout. He turned over the reins to his son Piero who immediately tried to shore up relations with Ludovico, but where Ludovico had taken a liking to Lorenzo, Piero lacked his father's charm. Ludovico was in fact a regent for Galeazzo's son Gian Galeazzo, but once he'd gained power Ludovico kept it, a *fait accompli* accepted by Gian Galeazzo who preferred hunting and was considered intellectually stunted. But Gian's wife was Isabella, granddaughter of King Ferrante of Naples, a perfect excuse for Ferrante to send troops to Milan to defend Isabella and Gian Galeazzo's right to the throne, whether Gian Galeazzo liked it or not.

Gian Galeazzo Maria Sforza was a veritable Renaissance beauty, about whom we will never know the truth. One reputable historian claims he was married at age 12 and father at age 14, but most historians maintain he married in 1469 at age 20, his bride age 18. They had four children, a girl who became Queen of Poland, a boy who was taken to France by Louis XII to learn kingship but died at age 20. Gian Galeazzo Maria was universally described as living in seclusion, well-guarded by men he repaid lavishly. Despite his guards and his wife's influence, his uncle murdered him, his age 25.

Ludovico requested the intervention of France which, due to its constant battles with England, had become the mightiest and most war-hardened army at the time. At its head rode Charles VIII, age 24. France considered itself the rightful possessor of Naples, but also of Milan. Ludovico's inviting him within the city walls was equivalent to his inviting a fox into the henhouse. Still, he had no choice, and so it was that two years after Lorenzo *Il Magnifico*'s death Charles entered Italy at the forefront of 60,000 men, the greatest invasion since Hannibal. Ludovico, quoted here, had no delusions about Charles: ''This King of France is young and of poor judgement; he is not advised as he ought to be. His advisors are in two groups: the one, and the other, absolutely opposed in all things to the first. In their determination to overcome each other, they have no care for the interests of the Kingdom. And each group is concerned with gaining money, with no care for anything else. All of them together would not make half of one competent man. When one, giving his attention to the matter for an instant, came to a decision and ordered that certain instructions be given, there was instantly another to cancel what the first had done. The King is haughty and ambitious beyond all imaging, and he has esteem for no one" (11).

Alexander had a plan of action against Charles VIII's invasion. He met with Alfonso II's son Ferdinand II, commonly known as Ferrandino, who would take troops into the Romagna and stop Charles from entering there. His brother Frederick would sail to Genoa, the destination of Charles' ships. Virginio Orsini promised to keep the French out of the north of Rome, the domain of the Orsini, while Alexander would do the same in the Papal States. But Charles' troops, many of whom were mercenaries, were heat-tempered professions, armed with cannons and the morality of beasts. They plundered, raped and murdered their way south, sending fear into the hearts of men and provoking the complete collapse of Alexander's plan of action. Frederick arrived too late to occupy Genoa and so he sailed on to Rapallo. Charles' Swiss mercenaries met him there and sacked and massacred the entire population, after which opposition to Charles in other city-states evaporated.

Charles was well received in Milan where, with his backing, Ludovico had Gian Galeazzo poisoned, although he spread the word that the young man had died from an excess of coitus. Then Charles fell nearly mortally ill with smallpox. When he miraculously recovered, his counselors suggested that he take control of Milan where he had been so wonderfully received, reminding him that thanks to marriages in earlier times the French had rights over Milan that were far stronger than those of a simple condottiere like Ludovico, this to the absolute horror of Ludovico himself. But Charles didn't have his mind on either Milan or Naples. What he wanted was Jerusalem, having promised God he would liberate the Holy City should he survive the smallpox. He saw himself not only in Jerusalem, but as liberator of Constantinople itself.

What shocked the Italians most about Charles was the mass destruction he brought into Italy, the first train of artillery ever seen, accompanied by barbarous Swiss mercenaries, the toughest and best-trained soldiers in the history of Europe. Towns were leveled and the survivors robbed and killed, the women raped. Until then Italy had known only condottieri, fighters of great value, men who preferred to take prisoners they could ransom, and avoided slaughter because the lord one fought against today, may be the lord who hired them tomorrow. The indiscriminant massacres of civilians would continue later under Louis XII, which inspired towns to give up without a fight, as both Charles and Louis knew they would.

In Florence Lorenzo's son Piero had sided with Naples, earning his expulsion from the city by Florentines who considered France a far richer market than Naples, a far better client for Florentine banks and manufacturing. This, plus the total destruction of the Florentine garrison of Fivizzano by French troops, tipped the scales against the Medici. Even so, when Charles entered Florence he was coldly received by the people. Piero felt he could make a comeback by seeking out Charles and throwing himself at Charles' feet, offering him free access to the town and, as gifts, Pisa and the port of Livorno. The Pisans were ecstatic because they hated the Florentines with every fiber of their bodies, but when they witnessed the sacking of Pisa and its environs, and the rape of their young girls by Charles' mercenaries, they realized their mistake. The dissident friar Savonarola made his way to Pisa where he welcomed the tyrant, calling him the godsend-liberator he had been predicting in his sermons. In Florence itself Charles told the people, with the breezy candor of his youth, that he cared nothing for them and the leaders they chose to rule them. What he wanted was money, and when he told them the amount they laughed in his face. Furious, Charles shouted that in that case he would sound his trumpets, to which the Florentines countered that they would sound their bell, the bell on the summit of the tower of the Palazzo della Signoria that would bring all the men of Florence and its surroundings running fully armed. Charles, wishing to get on to Naples unhampered, accepted their offer of 120,000 florins.

Savonarola.

The great Guicciardini in his marvelous *Storie fiorentini* tells us more about Savonarola: ''There were no more games in public, and even at home they were played in an atmosphere of fear. The taverns, which had been the meeting places for all the rowdy youth who enjoy every vice, were all closed up. Sodomy was ended and women abandoned showy and lascivious clothing, and young men resolved to live in a saintly and civilized way. They went to church regularly, wore their hair short and cast stones and cursed dishonest men, card players and women who dressed lewdly. They went to the carnival and collected all the dice, cards, paintings and corrupt books, and burned them publicly in the Piazza della Signoria. Savonarola brought help to men who abandoned pomp and vanities, and restricted themselves to the simplicity of a religious and Christian life.''

Before leaving Paris, Charles had entered into a number of extremely expensive treaties with kings such as Henry VII of England in order to cover his back should his engagement in Italy turn out to be more arduous than he had planned. As Naples belonged to the church, Charles needed Alexander's benediction to control it. But should Alexander prove recalcitrant, Charles was prepared to replace him with Cardinal della Rovere, the future Julius II, who was at his side, his wish to become pope only equal to his hatred of Alexander. In fact, counselors around the king tried to pursued him that Alexander had bought the papacy and was therefore not legitimate, and that the majority of the cardinals in Rome would thank Charles for rescuing the church by deposing him. Charles' stopover in Rome was the first test of Alexander's exceptional intelligence. Alexander nonetheless thought it a wise precaution to withdraw to the fortified Castel Sant'Angelo with all his possessions, including his bed. Charles tried to calm the Romans by telling them that his army wouldn't take an egg without paying for it. So numerous were his men that they took six hours to file through the gate of Santa Maria del Popolo, Giuliano della Rovere among the entourage. Charles took up residence in the Palazzo Venezia where he sat by the fire in slippers while his food was tasted by servants, his wine tested for poison, and the women sent to him closely inspected by those who knew his preferences. Charles, despite his extreme ugliness, had at least two different women a day, and in his baggage he carried a book of pornographic sketches and paintings of intercourse he had had with a few select beauties. His army may not have stolen a single egg, but it stole everything else that hadn't been battened down, reportedly cutting off fingers when rings refused to budge. His men raped any woman silly enough not to have fled the city. The palaces of the cardinals were especially prized, even those of Cesare and his mother. They killed as well, especially the Jews. They took any residence that pleased them, burning the furniture for warmth [Charles entered Rome in winter, on the 31st of December 1494], leaving the Palazzo Venezia, stated an observer, as dirty as a pigsty. Alexander finally agreed to a meeting that took place in the papal palace. Charles is reported to have rushed to him and was prevented from a third genuflection by the pope who stopped him in mid-kneeling, giving him the kiss of peace on the lips. As Charles and his troops had brought syphilis into Italy, the kiss could not have been hygienic.

Charles VIII.
He never had a woman more than once, and carried a collection of pornography in his baggage.
The French killed Jews, although ''Alexander was unusually tolerant. He viewed the Jews as fellow human beings who were simply mistaken in practicing a religion not wholly supported by true doctrine'' (11).

Syphilis may have been introduced into Europe by Christopher Columbus but this seems questionable as Columbus discovered the Americas in 1492 and the first cases of the disease were recorded in 1494 in Naples during Charles' invasion. How it could have spread so rapidly is one question, another question is why it wasn't present before Charles entered Naples, present in Paris for example. [At that time it was known, in French, as *le mal de Napoli.*] At any rate Charles had it and soon Cesare would be disfigured by its terrible scarification. Charles' unsanitary embrace of Alexander was an enormous victory for the pope whom Charles was thinking of deposing just a few days earlier, and an immense, albeit temporary, defeat for della Rovere. In fact, Charles and Alexander were seen riding through the country side-by-side, and walking through the Vatican gardens nearly arm-in-arm, Giuliano della Rovere smoldering in the shadows,

Alexander successfully bypassed Charles' request that he recognize his claim to Naples, a papal possession, as said, but the French king did insist on having Cesare as a traveling and hunting companion on his way to the city, with its magnificent view of the Bay of Naples and Vesuvius in the background--a hostage to make certain that the pope kept his troops in their barracks. Alfonso II of Naples abdicated in favor of his son Ferdinand II, affectionately called Ferrandino, Alfonso II ''almost catatonic with fear'' (3). Both fled Naples, leaving the city wide-open to Charles. On the way there Cesare hung back with his horse and then took French leave, Charles beside himself with fury. Another version has Cesare slipping away, disguised as a stable boy. But in both stories he left behind a treasure-trove in a covered wagon, Charles having insisted that he bring along enough wealth to prevent just this kind of incident. Charles' men immediately invested the wagon, finding, under the silk covering, trash. But Charles ended up forgiving Cesare as the boy had always fascinated him, and even in Paris Charles had pestered his ambassadors with questions about the lad. Cesare apparently could be a heathen when he chose, or charm personified when it suited his interests.

Charles entered Naples to wild cheers of ''*Francia! Francia!*'' Little did they suspect that the French would loot and rape wherever and whomever they wished, the whole paid for by a parting gift, the quasi-entirety of the population infected with syphilis.

There was nonetheless a fairy-book ending when Ferrandino was brought back to rule under the aegis of the Spanish, where he married a 17-year-old girl, Ferrandino 27.

Charles had made a mistake in accepting the 120,000 ducats offered by Florentines to get rid of him. This first proof of his fallibility--in tandem with the cruel, inhuman destruction of life and the raping of women--got Milan's Ludovico to thinking that he had made a mistake in inviting him into Italy. He entered into negotiations with Alexander and Venice, his mortal enemy, on how to stop the massacres. The Venetians, extremely well-armed, knew that Charles would eventually move against them, perhaps using Venetian fleets in his plans to invade the Holy Land. As for Ludovico, he was convinced that Charles would finally choose Milan to conquer over Jerusalem, the reason he solicited the help of Alexander and Venice, along with Siena, Urbino and Bologna, all of whom sent representatives to meet with Alexander. The result was the Holy League, led by Francesco II of Gonzaga under the direction of Alexander VI. It was the beginning of what became historically known as the First Italian War, which pitted the Holy Roman Empire, Spain and Italy against Charles VIII.

During this time Spain was silent but not inactive. Spain and France had signed the Treaty of Barcelona by which France bought Spain's neutrality by offering the Spanish two border provinces won by Charles' father Louis XI, at the cost of money and lives. But seeing Charles' unstoppable war machine and artillery, Ferdinand and Isabella sent ships and troops to Sicily.

They wouldn't have long to wait before entering Naples.

In face of such unity Charles was forced to retreat from Naples, although his power was intact enough to do grave damage to the anti-French coalition sent to fight him, costing the coalition 2,000 men to every 1,000 lost by Charles. The retreating French were nonetheless hounded by troops that attacked their baggage train until nothing remained to Charles of the tons of gold, jewels and other loot he had amassed. He and his Swiss and Gascon mercenaries massacred as they went, wiping Toscanella and Pontremoli off the map, while League soldiers harassed Charles through guerilla tactics. A battle did take place at Fornovo, where the fighting was vicious and thousands were killed, twice as many Italians as French. As for the dead on the battlefield, they were looted by their fellow soldiers and stripped naked of their clothing by peasants at night. On the day the Battle of Fornovo was fought, Spain captured Naples, welcomed by Neapolitans who had been mistreated by the French, while in Rome Alexander denounced the French for being worse than the Goths. He was now obliged to confront the Spanish, the equivalent of jumping from the frying pan into the fire.

''Apart from a very small number of cultivated and moral people, Spaniards are uncultivated and desire to remain so; they have no aspiration for learning; they feel no need either of refinement of manners or improvement of life. The young people are not educated to this end but, on the contrary, are degraded; for instead of sending them, as is done in the rest of Europe, to be prepared for life by people of nobler condition, they are kept with their own inferiors, who teach them all the ways of evil. Among them it is a virtue to know how to deceive and to rob one's neighbor with skill and cunning. They are pompous and sensitive to affront; barbarians, and like all barbarians, lustful; old and young sing beneath their mistresses' windows,'' an unknown commentator (11).

In a way, worse awaited Charles at Poggibonsi where Savonarola scurried to tell him that he had failed because he hadn't accomplished the will of God; he hadn't cleansed Italy of its filth in the form of the pope and his bastards; he hadn't fulfilled his promise to liberate Jerusalem; and if Charles didn't listen to the word of God that passed through the mouth of his chosen servant Savonarola, God would replace him with someone who would, which the Lord did two years later by fracturing Charles' head against a doorframe as he was rushing off to play tennis, causing him to hemorrhage to death.

As for Alexander VI, he had defeated a king who had had immense wealth and the biggest army of his day, and had given Charles nothing other than the red hat of a cardinal for the king's cousin Philip of Luxembourg.

G.J. Meyer points out that the invasion should have taught Italy that its survival depended on its being united. But this was far from the case, as each city-state and each great family changed sides when profit beckoned, or when they felt it was in their military interest to do so. Strangely, only one pure value came through, like unalterably gold, the steadfastness of a certain Alexander VI.

Alexander wrote to Savonarola: "We are displeased at the disturbed state of affairs in Florence, the more so in that it owes its origin to your preaching. For you predict the future and publicly declare that you do so by the inspiration of the Holy Spirit when you should be reprehending vice and praising virtue. Such prophecies may easily lure the simple-minded away from the path of salvation and the obedience due to the Holy Roman Church. Prophecies like these should not be made when your charge is to forward peace and concord. Moreover, these are not the time for such teachings, calculated as they are to produce discord even in times of peace let alone in times of trouble. Since, however, we have been most happy to learn from certain cardinals and from your letter that you are ready to submit yourself to the reproofs of the Church, as becomes a Christian and a religious, we are beginning to think that what you have done has not been done with an evil motive, but from a certain simple-mindedness and a zeal, however misguided, for the Lord's vineyard. Our duty, however, prescribes that we order you, under holy obedience, to cease from public and private preaching until you are able to come to our presence, not under armed escort as is your present habit, but safely, quietly and modestly as becomes a religious, or until we make different arrangements. If you obey, as we hope you will, we for the time being suspend the operation of our former Brief so that you may live in peace in accordance with the dictates of your conscience."

CHAPTER SEVEN

THE DEATH OF JUAN BORGIA

1497

Cesare was described by the great Boccaccio, author of *The Decameron*--a book as wonderful today as then--as possessed of genius and charm, lively and merry and happy in the company of society. He was also ambition to the extreme and fearless--in fact, like his father Alexander, he feared nothing and no one. Cesare addressed Juan as his Lord brother, and admonished him to give thanks to their father His Holiness, who had made the family so great. Juan was married in Barcelona to a young cousin of King Ferdinand and Queen Isabella. Given everything he could wish for from birth, Juan spent his time whoring--and his young body was capable of giving him a great deal of pleasure--drinking and gambling. It's not known if he honored his wife on their wedding night, so decided was he to go off with his friends to shatter the quiet of the Barcelona night. ''Juan was too busy spending time in brothels to consummate his marriage, besotted by many kinds of depravities'' (11).

Juan was clearly Alexander's favorite, another supposed reason for Cesare's hatred. As virile as his father, slim waisted and certain of his sex appeal, Juan swaggered through the streets of Rome in what can only be described as gorgeous attire, a black cloak of gold brocade, jewel-encrusted waistcoats and silk shirts, skin-tight trousers with drop-fronts--held in place by ribbons he detached when he wished to piss and fuck. This beautiful, gorgeously clad body, stabbed nine times, 30 golden ducats still in his belt purse, was fished up from the Tiber, to the grief-stricken horror of his father who locked himself away from public view for three days. The death freed the way for Cesare to renounce his vows as cardinal. Alexander never confronted his son with the murder of his favorite boy, but that he was guilty was silently acknowledged by nearly all. On the morning of the murder, just before sunrise, men had been seen leading a horse with a body strapped over its back to the river edge, untie and then cast it into the middle. They were accompanied by another man on a white charger, his silver stirrups and gold spurs reflecting the moon's glow. The men, said the witness, a Slovenian watchman standing guard over boats carrying cargo, spoke in very low voices ... in Spanish.

On the night of June 1st 1497 Juan and his brother Cesare had dined at their mother Vannozza's palace, after which they rode off together, but separated when Juan told Cesare he had other pleasures in mind elsewhere. Juan was accompanied by a servant who was discovered in a pool of blood at dawn the next morning, nothing surprising as a dozen victims of robberies and vendettas were found each morning on the streets of Rome. Nor did Juan's absence from the Vatican raise alarm, as he was known to participate in drunken orgies that lasted a week. Only when he was brought up in a fisherman's net three days later, wrote Burchard, did Alexander succumb ''to grief and anguish, weeping most bitterly'' (7).

Given Cesare's continual disputes with his brother, and the fact that he had been the last known person to have seen him alive, he was more than suspected.

Yet people other than Cesare have also been mentioned as possible murderers, one of whom was Jofrè. It's not clear at exactly what age Jofrè married but he was thought to be 12 and his wife Sancia 16. As puberty was far later in the Renaissance than today [possibly as late as ages 15 or 16] he was unwilling to consummate the union, his testosterone levels too low to inspire the necessary lust. His brothers took over the task for him, however, an experience that was not necessarily grueling for the young girl as she was rumored to have had many lovers before arriving in Rome. At any rate, some historians place their bet on Jofrè as his brother's assassin, out of jealously, Juan who had taken Jofrè's place on Jofrè's wedding night, to the joy of Sancia who loved his slim virile body, and so close were the brothers that it is not impossible that Jofrè was present, Juan demonstrating what would be expected of him later. With puberty came the realization of the extent to which Juan had made a fool of him, a secret that should have remained between the brothers but one that Juan couldn't help bragging about, the consequence of which was Jofrè's hatred for the warrior brother he had until then worshipped. Yet in reality, Jofrè played only a minor role in the uncoiling events attached to the Borgia. He was made Prince of Squillace, a vassal town of Naples where he lived until he died, having produced four children of his own. Jofrè seems to have been a loving prince, certainly a lucky one as he was the center of attention in Squillace, attended by scores of servants, and for a boy who was so calm and steady, a wife like Sancia may have added spice to his otherwise tranquil existence.

Cardinal Ascanio Sforza was also suspected of killing Juan as he had had a clash with the boy for unknown reasons, although few reasons were necessary for the headstrong Juan to pick fights with everyone. Ascanio wrote to his brother: ''The uncertainty has given rise to many conjectures. Some think it had to do with a love affair. Some believe my people have done it, on account of a recent quarrel with the duke. Finally, some think that either Giovanni Sforza or his brother Galeazzo is the murderer'' (7).

In the same vein, Carl Orsini was also accused because he too had had a falling out with Juan, sending him a vile message wedged in the anus of a donkey.

Others thought the murderer was Lucrezia's husband Giovanni Sforza. Even before his marriage to Lucrezia, Giovanni had learned that his wife had had sexual congress with both her brothers Cesare and Juan, as well as her father Alexander, or so it was rumored, rumors gaining in lewdness with each retelling. Giovanni wished to destroy them all, as a way of avenging his humiliation at having been made a fool of. Again, the accusations of incest were based on nothing more than rumors, and as author Rafael Sabatini put it so well, historians were ready to accept any nonsense as long as it was ''well-salted and well-spiced''. [Alas, there is no adequate painting of Juan.]

When Alexander came out of mourning he announced to the Council of Cardinals, ''The Duke of Gandía is dead. A greater calamity could not have befallen us for we bore him unbounded affection. Life has lost all interest for us. It must be that God punishes us for our sins, for the Duke has done nothing to deserve so terrible a fate'' (2).

It will never be known if Alexander suspected his son Cesare of committing the irreparable. Juan had been deeply and sincerely loved by his father, but his sudden disappearance, and what suspicions he had, did nothing to lessen the tandem he continued to form with Cesare. That Alexander ceased to search for his boy's murderer could mean that in his heart he knew, or it could have been similar to the loss of Jack Kennedy, whose inseparable brother Robert wanted to know nothing of the person who had forever deprived him of his companion.

Alexander VI
''When Alexander heard that the duke had been murdered and his body thrown like carrion into the Tiber, he was perfectly overcome; he shut himself in his room overwhelmed with grief and wept bitterly,'' a quote from Burchard in Marion Johnson's *The Borgia*.

A week before Juan's assassination Cesare, still a cardinal, had gone to Naples to crown Frederick of Aragon, King of Naples [also known as Frederick IV].

Frederick was the brother of Alfonso II, Afonso II who fathered Sancia, **Jofrè**'s wife, and a son, another Alfonso, soon to marry Lucrezia. The psychopath Ferrante had fathered Alfonso II, who abdicated in favor of his son Ferdinand II, called Ferrandino, who died of fever at age 27 [at a time when life expectancy was age 30]. The throne then went to Frederick.

While in Naples, Cesare convinced Frederick to give Alfonso II's 18-year-old son to Lucrezia, Alfonso of Aragon, Sancia's brother. [In the Showtime *The Borgias*, Alfonso is still virgin, a huge attraction to Lucrezia who was generous with so many, but given Renaissance mores, Alfonso could have been heterosexually chaste only if he was homosexually active.] Juan Borgia wasn't forgotten. Frederick appointed him head of Neapolitan troops, at a yearly 33,000 ducats, although he wouldn't be obliged to step foot into the city. Christopher Hibbert states that it was rumored that Sancia wanted to give up Cesare's brother **Jofrè in exchange for Cesare, an annulment based on Jofrè** becoming a cardinal and Cesare replacing Juan at the head of the pope's troops, a reason for his killing Juan a week later, a scenario as byzantine as were the Borgia themselves, but it is highly unlikely that Cesare cared enough about easily-accessible Sancia to consider, for a nanosecond, marriage to her.

1498

As said, Savonarola had welcomed Charles with open arms, claiming that he had asked God to send the Frenchman as an arm to punish the evildoers in Italy in general, and Florence in particular. He had then dismissed the king like a servant. He himself replaced Charles with gangs of boys he sent to scour the city of its whorehouses, its licentious taverns, its musical instruments, its card games and, especially, its sodomists. When Savonarola had first come to Florence he had gained a huge following because he had had the right answers to how Florentines could wage war against corruption, brigands and iniquity. He painted a clear picture of the depravity of the church, from the trading of indulgences to the selling of cardinal hats. He was the precursor of the coming Reformation, and because he was ahead of his time he was burned at the stake.

Detail of Savonarola burned at the stake, artist unknown.

Despite the fact that Cesare had murdered his brother and Alexander's favorite son, Juan, both father and the remaining son, Cesare, stayed united, the purpose of which was to extend Alexander's power and to give Cesare enough strength so that he would be able to replace the pope, at his death, becoming the first ruler of a unified Italy since the Romans.

Also in 1498 Louis XII sent carefully chosen ambassadors to the Vatican for the purpose of inviting Cesare to France, with a letter signed by Louis, naming Cesare Duke of Valence. Like Louis' father Charles VIII, Louis too was intrigued by Cesare's reputation, although Louis, a brilliant monarch, had far deeper reasons to court the Borgia, just as he had, financially, infinitely deeper pockets and an infinitely grander army. ''The King publicly embraced and welcomed him with great joy and led him into the castle where he had him installed in the chamber nearest his own, and the King himself ordered his supper, choosing diverse dishes and he ordered that his guest should dress in the King's own shirt and tunic. In short, he could not have done more for a son or a brother,'' stated a witness (2).

It was under these highly favorable auspicious that Alexander arranged a rapprochement between Louis XII of France and the Vatican. This the pope accomplished thanks to three of the new king's needs: the need to conquer Milan, his possession due to a grandmother who had married a Visconti, one of Milan's first rulers; the need to reconquer Naples, lost with the death of Charles VIII; and the need for a divorce so that Louis could marry Charles' widow, a renowned beauty. Louis offered Alexander a huge sum of money and gave Cesare, whom all recognized as the new rising star, command over several thousand French troops. Satisfied, Alexander threw in a cardinal's hat that the French had requested for years. Not to be outdone, Louis raised the stakes by offering to find Cesare a noble wife. Alexander's rapprochement paid off in spades. Thanks to French intervention in Italy, the four greats would be neutered: Florence and Bologna would become client states of France, doing Louis' bidding in exchange for his protection against Cesare; Venice would be neutralized by the offer of some territorial scraps when Louis conquered Milan; and Milan itself would be French.

When Cesare realized that he would soon be meeting Louis in person, he decided to turn himself into a perfect male by force of exercise, physical exercise as well as exercise in arms and horsemanship. He spent hours at the task and contemporaries agreed that there was not a finer looking Italian in all of Italy. Cesare's good looks were increasingly disfigured by the ravages of syphilis. The syphilitic rashes, euphemistically called ''flowers'', came and went like the tide, leaving him handsome or disfigured *selon*. He took to wearing masks during his bad days, the effect of which enhanced the fear people already had of him.

When the time came, Cesare set off for France with cartloads of precious gifts. He was beautifully dressed in black and white velvet, pearls and gold chains and precious gems attached to his clothes and boots, his horse attired in gorgeous livery and silver bells. He was accompanied by dozens of mules covered in satin, in cloth of gold, dozens of grooms in crimson velvet, noblemen in gold and silver, musicians playing trumpets, all of which made the French laugh at his pomposity. He knelt to kiss Louis' foot but was halted and allowed the king's hand instead. In addition to the wealthy display, Cesare had not forgotten the cardinal's hat to be presented to Georges d'Amboise, Louis' trusted counselor. Cesare was offered the sister of the King of Navarre, sixteen-year-old Charlotta d'Albret. Alexander was hoping for a better match for his son, a girl from the king's own family, but allowed the marriage because Cesare seemed happy with her, and Alexander even gave the girl's brother, Amanieu d'Albret, a cardinal's hat. Louis wrote Alexander a description of the wedding night, telling the pope that Cesare honored his wife eight times in a row. Louis added that he had done the same with his new wife-- thanks to the divorce Alexander had accorded him--but confessed that he had nonetheless done less well as his sessions had been broken up, twice before dinner, six times afterwards. Alexander replied that he was awed by the king and proud of his son but not surprised by his virility. Carlotta was immediately pregnant with a girl, Cesare's only known child. Charles' former wife wasn't. Louis' first wife entered a nunnery and was canonized in 1950. From here on, Cesare put the French coat-of-arms, the fleur-de-lys, on all his possessions, accompanied by the Borgia bull.

CHAPTER EIGHT

THE CAPTURE OF CATERINA SFORZA

The Jubilee of 1500 opened its doors in 1499. The Jubilee was founded by Pope Boniface XIII in 1300 as a means of filling church coffers, thanks to alms received in exchange for the forgiveness of sins committed by the thousands of pilgrims that flocked to Rome, the whole given the appearance of legitimacy thanks to fasting, prayer, confession and communion. At its origin it was scheduled for each century, but Paul II decided, in 1470, that once every 25 years would be more beneficial to church finances. Veritable casks were provided for the reception of offerings, stated Burchard, to which three keys existed, each held by a different person. The churches were swept clean during the period and loiterers hauled away.

Alexander ordered a very special event for his Jubilee. The Holy Door of St. Peter's would be opened, a door that Emperor Vespasian had brought from Jerusalem, through which Christ himself had entered the Holy City, through which, during the Jubilee, anyone passing under was forgiven his sins, even murderers.

On the 24th of December 1499 Alexander struck at the mortar sealing the door with three blows from a hammer, and then retired to his chair while workmen, entertained by a singing choir of boys, removed the rest of the cement. Alexander, in full robes and tiara, then entered, followed by the college of cardinals. [Workmen, states Burchard, had been warned that they would lose their heads if any part of their anatomy passed the door before the pope's entry.]

Caterina Sforza by Lorenzo di Credi.

But the greatest event of 1499 was the destruction of **Forlì** and the capture of Caterina Sforza, a huge segment of the Showtime *The Borgias* dedicated to this unique person, easily on a par with Eleanor of Aquitaine and Catherine de' Medici.

Caterina Sforza was the daughter of Galeazzo Maria Sforze covered in Chapter Three. That Caterina Sforza was illegitimate was of no consequence in the Italy of the Renaissance. In that, Italy was totally exceptional. Not only was Caterina treated with the same love as her legitimate brothers and sister, she was offered the same education as the boys in the palace, unlike what girls were offered in most other parts of the country. In addition to a superb education, she learned to handle arms, to ride and to hunt. She was a Sforza, born into a family of warriors that dated back to Francisco Sforza, her grandfather. She was thusly the daughter of Francisco Sforza's son, Galeazzo Maria Sforza, whom she adored, and the mother she loved, Lucrezia Landriani. Caterina was destined to be married three times and through each of them she would proudly wear the Sforza name. Her love for her father continued untainted even when, at age ten, she was betrothed to Girolamo Riario, count of Imola, who insisted on deflowering her despite the tradition that the girls should be at least fourteen. Girolamo had been offered another girl, age eleven, but her family backed out as soon as they learned of Girolamo's pedophilic tendencies. Girolamo was continuously described at depraved by contemporary historians without further details--although the reason may simply have been his taste for virgins and a huge capacity for women in general. Caterina's wedding night may have been rough [as her adored father certainly knew it would be], but thereafter she was known for her numerous sexual encounters and her attraction to especially handsome lads, one of whom, a stable boy, she raised to lord of Forlì after her husband Girolamo's death. She would eventually present Girolamo with six sons and a daughter. Girolamo was the son of a shoemaker whose good luck was to have Pope Sixtus IV, known for his nepotism, for uncle. Thanks to Sixtus, Caterina became countess of Imola and Forlì.

Two paintings of Girolamo Riario who deflowered Caterina at age 10 with her beloved father's consent.

Caterina decided to leave Imola for a short visit to her mother, sister and relatives in Milan. There, to her stupefaction, she found a city in full bloom thanks to the new ruler Ludovico Sforza who had opened Milan to engineers, architects and artists. In fact, the city was being rebuild from the foundations up. The most famous Sforza acquisition was young Leonardo da Vince whom everyone found gorgeous--slim, strong, physically powerful and possessing cascades of hair flowing around his beautiful face. Caterina anticipated a close relationship by offering the boy a commission to do her portrait. Alas for her, this boy preferred other boys.

A reconstruction of what da Vinci looked like.

Back home in Forlì, Caterina became more and more aware of her husband's unpopularity. She realized that if something happened to Girolamo she would survive only if she were in absolute command of the Ravaldino fortress, said to be impregnable. But the fortress had a particularity. When someone was designated to man it, he was given absolute powers in its defense, and was never allowed to go beyond its walls. At the moment the fortress was held by a certain Zaccheo, a person who had bought the job from Girolamo who was always in need of money. Caterina knew she couldn't trust him to turn the fortress over to her in time of great need. Her first priority, therefore, was to put someone else in his place. She rode to Ravaldino, "pregnant to the throat," said Zaccheo when he saw her. Zaccheo told her that he could be replaced only by Girolamo himself, not some woman, be she even a countess and Girolamo's wife. Caterina returned to Forlì and engaged the help of a man who was Zaccheo's only friend, a sinister personage named Codronchi. Codronchi went to Ravaldino and was welcomed by Zaccheo. While awaiting dinner they played cards. When one slipped from Zaccheo's hands and he bent to retrieve it, Codronchi reached for a dagger in the top of his boot and brought it up into Zaccheo's heart, killing him instantly. The man's body was dumped down a well and Ravaldino was turned over to Caterina. Codronchi rode away from Forlì, much richer. Tommaso Feo, a stable boy Caterina amused herself with, was chosen to govern the fortress. He came with his brother Giacomo, 15, whom Caterina took an even greater shine to and … later married.

Ravaldino

Things boiled over, and what Caterina had expected finally happened. One of the noble clans, the Orsi, had had enough of Girolamo. As close friends of his, they were allowed to enter the palace early one afternoon while Girolamo was resting, and knifed him. Girolamo was able to raise himself and attempted to get to Caterina's rooms but the Orsi brothers kept slashing with daggers until he lay in a pool of his own blood. The body was thrown over the balcony into the piazza where Forlivesi examined the mangled remains and bloody face. At first fearful, they turned on it once they knew the tyrant was truly dead. He was kicked, spat upon and beaten. The Forlivesi then sacked the palace, taking away everything, down to the bedding. The Orsi ran to Caterina's apartments where she was entertaining her mother, sister and children. The children broke into terrified sobs, only Girolamo's bastard son, Scipione, age fourteen, faced the attackers with bravado. They were all locked in but luckily Caterina was able to get a message out to Naples and Bologna, as well as to the new pope, Innocent VIII in Rome. Bishop Savelli, who happened to be touring the region, entered Forlì the next day and immediately, on learning what was going on, went to make sure that nothing had happened to Caterina and her children. As the population knew that she could count on the huge armies of both Milan and Bologna, neither it nor the Orsi dared harm her. In addition, the mighty fortification of Ravaldino was now in the hands of a man loyal to the countess.

Whether Bishop Savelli was in league with Caterina or not is unknown. What is known is that he accompanied her to the fortification of Ravaldino that she promised to hand over to the Orsi. The keeper, who was in league with her, said he would do so if she would pay his back wages and ensure his future employment there or elsewhere. When she agreed, he said she would have to enter the fortification and give him what he wanted in writing. The Orsi rejected the idea until Bishop Savelli vouched for her integrity. She entered Ravaldino, the door closed behind her, she mounted the steps to the top of the tower where she gave the Orsi-- the finger.

The Orsi, outraged, went back to the palace where they fetched her son Ottaviano, age nine. He was brought back before the walls of Ravaldino and a dagger was placed against the lad's throat, the worst possible nightmare for a mother. The child was obliged to cry out for mercy, alerting Caterina to his presence. She returned to the top of the tower and stared down at the Orsi, their troops and the town people who had desecrated the body of her husband and ransacked her palace. She felt she had little to fear as they were all deathly afraid of the consequences of their acts. Spies had already returned to Forlì to inform them that troops from Bologna and Milan were on their way, and they all knew too that the new pope would never accept that even a hair of any of the children be harmed.

Accordingly, Caterina hollered out the words that have made her famous to this day. She told them they could do what they would with her children as she was pregnant again and with *this*, she added, pointing to her loins, she could produce many others. Galeotto Manfredi, a friend of Lorenzo *Il Magnifico* de' Medici, sent a letter to Lorenzo in which he stated that, in fact, Caterina had hiked up her skirt and, pointing to her bare ''cunt'', wrote Galeotto, had bellowed out her famous words. The Orsi retreated as troops in favor of Caterina neared, and Caterina resumed power.

It was doing this period that Caterina is believed to have sent a personal message to Alexander, wrapped in a fabric that had been worn by a victim of the plague, an attempt that failed.

As said, Caterina had had her eye on a stable boy, Giacomo Feo, since he was fifteen. Now seventeen, tall, lithe and supranormally handsome, his contemporaries tell us he was big where it counted. When Caterina found herself pregnant, she secretly married the kid.

All hell broke out in every direction. Forlivesi and Imolesi couldn't accept the primacy of a stable boy over their cities, and Bologna, Milan, Florence and Ferrara proclaimed that they had youths of noble birth who could satisfy the countess at least as well as Feo. The city that eventually won out, should Caterina choose one of their boys, would not only broaden its territory thanks to its influence over the two city-states, but it would control a major artery through the Apennines. Foiled attempts were made on the lives of both the countess and her lad, but she brought her pregnancy to term, giving birth to a baby boy, Bernardino. A visiting ambassador was allowed into the inner sanctum of Caterina's palace where she and Giacomo were playing with Catherina's children by Girolamo and her son by Feo. He described the husband and wife, in the light of the setting sun, as pure angels.

Giacomo Feo, the stable boy, now decided politics for the two city-states, certain that he knew as much or more than seasoned kings, counts, ambassadors and other diplomats. But Caterina's son Ottaviano, age 16, was now a man. In an attempt to gain what was his, he went up to his mother and Feo and demanded to be recognized as the new count of Forlì and Imola. An argument ensued that ended with Feo slapping the boy, who stormed out of the room red-faced. A week later, as Feo was riding through the woods along with

Caterina, a group of friends approached them on horse. While Feo chatted amiably with one, another stuck a dagger in his back. Caterina had the presence of mind to turn and ride off to the impregnable shelter of Ravaldino. Feo's bodyguards also took flight, leaving the handsome boy to fall from his horse into a ditch.

The people of Forlì remembered the heads Caterina ordered cut off after the assassination of Girolama. So when the murderers of Feo came riding into the town square, their clothes filthy with his blood, shouting to all the account of their exploits which, they maintained, were designed to give power over Forlì and Imola to their rightful count, Ottaviano, a group of nobles thought best to go to Ravaldino to find out what had really happened. When they returned, they ordered the arrest of the assassins. The reprisals were indeed terrible. The murderers had their heads axed open, from the top to the chin. Their wives and mistresses and children were slaughtered. Their houses were torn down brick by brick. Two babies associated with them, age three and nine months, along with their nurses, were bludgeoned to death. An accused priest was dragged behind a horse, his head fractured against the cobblestones. Under torture another conspirator gave out the name of her son Ottaviano, known by all to have hated Feo for usurping his rightful place as count of Forlì and Imola. Caterina had her son arrested, an act so horrifying that the inhabitants followed the boy to the gates of Ravaldino where Caterina dispersed them with cannon fire. At Feo's funeral all of Forlì and Imola turned out, so afraid were the populations of their countess. Heaven entered the act by bringing down a plague on the people: rashes appeared on their genitals and their lymph nodes swelled up. The syphilis epidemic had begun. Caterina ordered her palace torn down because it had sheltered both her and Feo, and his statue in bronze was raised in his honor. A new palace was build on the grounds of fortified Ravaldino. Its furnishings and gardens were so exquisite that Caterina called it Paradise. She sent Ottaviano to Florence to learn the art of war. The sixteen-year-old lad, a veritable Don Juan like his father Girolamo, left behind mistresses and bastards.

Caterina had eight children. Bianca Riario was her only girl and Caterina destined her for handsome Astorre Manfredi, lord of neighboring Faenza. For Caterina, marital bliss occurred much sooner. At age thirty-three she fell in love with Giovanni de' Medici, thirty, perhaps the first veritably educated man in her life, who was also handsome and charming and, said one wag, a boy for whom she would kill father and mother to keep near her. Alas, her new husband Giovanni had inherited, in spades, the ills of his ancestors: he died in Caterina's arms, probably of complications due to family gout.

Two supposed portraits of Giovanni de' Medici

Pope Alexander VI decided the time had come to bring Forlì and Imola into the lap of the Papal States. His son Cesare arrived at Ravaldino at the head of an army of twelve thousand. After promising her money and a palace of her own in Rome, the tone between the two--Cesare on his white charger facing the drawbridge to Ravaldino, Caterina atop the crenellated tower--turned sour as one insulted the other. They split up but after a few hours of reflection Cesare returned. This time Caterina was standing on the drawbridge. Cesare dismounted and approached the edge. Handsome and gorgeously dressed in black velvet, a rarity during the period when both sexes preferred bright colors [after the austerity of the Middle Ages], he decided to trade the filthy language he was partial to with the troops for the sparkling oratory of the likes of Cicero. Caterina too was in beauty, her breasts propped up by a tight bodice. She was immediately aware that Cesare had come to seduce her with a stunning smile similar to that used by Stanley Kowalski to mollify his wife Stella. Caterina, with the same intention, turned a welcoming shoulder in his direction, he held out a hand to touch it, she enticingly took a step back in the direction of the door to Ravaldino, he followed ... until he felt the drawbridge rising under his feet. He jumped off just in time to see Caterina disappear behind the closing door. Cesare, his face red with shame for having been tricked, stormed off.

Sadly, Cesare would win out. What Caterina had pointed to when the Orsi had put a dagger against the throat of her son when ordering her to surrender Ravaldino, what Galeotto had referred to as her ''cunt'' in a letter, would soon be not only his, but his until he himself felt that his humiliation of her had gone on long enough. [Although some writers during the period suggested that she grew to *like* Cesare and his form of humiliation. Naturally, we'll never ever know.]

For the moment, Cesare went back to his obscene military language and ordered an all-out attack on the citadel. I won't go into the actual destruction except to say that she was betrayed from inside the walls, walls opened to Cesare and his French troops. The Italians inside were spared but ransomed; the mercenaries under Caterina had their throats slit. She stepped over seven hundred strewn corpses on her way out of Ravaldino, in time to see her monument of bronze to her beloved Feo being carted away prior to being melted into cannon balls. Feo was symptomatic of what had undermined her place in Forlì and Imola: she had fought for her own pleasure and a place in the sun for her children; she had known dozens of lads and wealth and luxury beyond measure; and so as one citizen summed it all up as she was hauled away, ''She had put her faith in herself and in the walls of her fortress, and none in the people she ruled.''

The French troops with Cesare observed the fate of the women left behind, their thighs spread as the men lined up. They knew that the prettiest had already been put aside for themselves later on. Realizing what was in store for Caterina, several tried to save the countess by telling Cesare that they had precedence over her and would assure her safety right up to the moment she came before King Louis XII. This hiatus ended in an exchange of money. Cesare retired with the countess while the French officers, rich, sought the comfort of the naked forms awaiting them under the covers of their own beds. One of them was heard to say, as he unbuttoned his superb military tunic, ''Well, at least she won't be wanting for fucking.''

Caterina was imprisoned in the Castel Sant'Angelo. She was said to have deeply regretted those she had murdered after the assassinations of Girolamo and Feo, a score for the first, two score for the second. Life supposedly meant little at the time, yet I remain convinced that individuals during the Renaissance wanted to live out their lives, just as we do today, to the last moment. They certainly were barbarous, hanging people until they were nearly dead and then cutting them down, still alive, so they could watch themselves be disemboweled or have their hearts cut out still beating, or, the horror of horrors, have their privates cut away and stuffed in their mouths to suffocate on. The rape of women was an essential perk of war, as was ransacking and destruction. So Caterina had reason to repent and beg for God's forgiveness, and we certainly have reason to be thankful for our own more civilized times ... if, naturally, one excludes the Great War responsible for 20,000,000 deaths, the Second that caused twice that, and, more recently the slaughter of 8,000 boys from age 13 in Srebrenica, all of whom certainly begged for their precious lives right up to the last horrifying second.

Caterina was locked away, out of the reach of those like Cesare and his close friends who would be able to crow over having possessed the charms of the Cleopatra who hadn't gotten away. Her pain deepened when she discovered that her sons, Ottaviano and Cesare, were doing just fine under the rule of Alexander, from whom both boys sought the red hat of a cardinal. With mistresses and bastards galore, they were certainly on the right path to seeing their wishes fulfilled. News from Florence informed her that her last husband's brother was dilapidating the fortune Giovanni de' Medici had willed to her and his son, little Giovanni.

At age ten Caterina had visited Florence with her father Galeazzo Marie Sforza and had been welcomed by Lorenze *Il Magnifico* himself. Thanks to the intervention of Louis XII, who respected her as a ruler and as a warrior, she was freed from Castel Sant'Angelo--after signing over Forlì and Imola to Alexander. As she left the castel she crossed paths with Astorre Mandredi who was being imprisoned. The year of his imprisonment was 1501, his story to follow. She made her way back to Florence, the most beautiful and cultivated city of the Renaissance, where she would die. In an ending that was almost a fairytale of beauty, she was met there by her sons Ottaviano, Cesare, Scipione, Galeazzo, Sforzino and Bernardino--the son of Feo. Her only daughter, the loyal Bianca, was also waiting for her, holding in her arms little Giovanni, the son of her last love, Giovanni de' Medici, whose fortune his brother had not entirely dilapidated--in fact, there remained enough so that Caterina could live in comfort and offer sums to her sons who never ever stopped making requests for this and that, just as they had, when infants, lustily and eagerly suckled at the breasts of their wet-nurses.

To save her soul she made donations to convents and churches, especially to the convent of Muratte where she asked to be interred. These donations were to Christ, for it is to Christ that women turn when they are no longer of an age to welcome virile lovers. She passed away at age forty-six. The year was 1509. Her tomb was desecrated 300 years later and her remains lost when Muratte became a prison.

But before we finish with Caterine, perhaps a word about her last son, little Giovanni. Different from the other Medici, he spurned intellectual activities in favor of martial interests. He often ran away from home and liked the company of simple farm boys. At age twelve he killed a boy and at age thirteen he raped a boy of sixteen. Trying desperately to save him, Florentine nobles put him under the control of an ambassador, Salviati, who was named to Rome. There Giovanni slummed with lowlifes, in perpetual trouble. He became a condottiere and was known for exclaiming, ''I rule with my ass in the saddle and a sword in my fist!'' Pope Leo X chose him first to police Rome and then to form an army using men of normally irredeemable depravity that only Giovanni had the force to make into manageable soldiers. He specialized in lightning strikes with a preference for ambushes, stating, ''I embrace my rivals in order to strangle them''. When his patron Pope Leo X died, Giovanni added black stripes to his armor, for which he is known historically as Giovanni dalle Bande Nere. He married Salviati's daughter and had a son destined to become lord of Florence. Severely wounded in battle, he had to have his foot amputated; ten men were needed to hold him down. He died five days later of gangrene. He was the very last of the condottieri. Of his direct descendants--other than fathering a Florentine lord--one, Marie de' Medici, became Queen of France [but led a terribly sorrowful life]. The Florentine lord he sired was Cosimo I who would rule Florence (7), employ Michelangelo, and encourage Cellini to give birth to a miracle equal to Michelangelo's *David*, Cellini's *Perseus* (5).

Giovanni dalle Bande Nere

While Louis XII was pressing forward with his plans to capture Milan and Naples, he realized that Spain, under Ferdinand and Isabella, would seize the opportunity of his being away in Italy to invade France. He therefore signed an agreement with Spain, the Treaty of Granada, that promised to divide the spoils of Naples between France and Spain, a document accepted by Alexander VI, signed in 1501. Louis had rights to Milan due to family heritage, but had no right to Naples except that Naples had been conquered by Charles VIII, who had bequeathed it to France. In 1504 Louis XII and Ferdinand II of Spain signed the Treaty of Lyon, under which Spain received Naples and control over southern Italy, France received Milan and control over northern Italy.

On the 28th of September Alexander gained control over his dissident cardinals by appointing 13 new cardinals to the College of Cardinals. An incredible event, but a drop in the bucket to the 43 new cardinals he would name during his pontificate.

Now that Alexander and Cesare were aligned with France against Milan and Naples, Lucrezia's husband Alfonso, illegitimate son of the former king of Naples Alfonso II, was an embarrassment that the two men eliminated by eliminating Alfonso himself. The boy had dined with the pope and was on his way home when waylaid by men with daggers. Wounded, he was taken to the Vatican where the pope gave him his own rooms.

Instinctively knowing what was in store for the lad she loved, Lucrezia hovered over him day and night. Alfonso knew who was responsible for his injuries, and when he had recuperated enough, he took a potshot at Cesare with a crossbow as he passed through the garden below Alfonso's window. Cesare was unscathed, but his reaction was immediate. He sent men to clear Alfonso's rooms of both Alfonso's sister, Sancia, and his wife, Lucrezia. When they refused to budge, the men told the women that they were acting under orders from the pope himself. If the two women doubted their word they could ask the pope who was in an adjoining apartment. As they left to do so, the doors to Alfonso's rooms were closed and Alfonso strangled, probably by Micheletto de Corella, Cesare's loyal assassin. Cesare made no pretense of innocence, maintaining that since Alfonso had tried to kill him, he was only protecting his life. Micheletto was rewarded by being made governor of Rome, a position that gave him extraordinary access to money.

Despite Lucrezia's efforts to save her, Sancia was imprisoned in the Castel Sant'Angelo until the death of Alexander, as the court needed to get rid of the symbol of Cesare's crime. When freed she returned to her native Naples where she was visited by Cesare who brought her Lucrezia's child by Pedro Calderon to raise, which she agreed to do. She died of natural causes in 1506 at age 27, a year after Cesare.

CHAPTER NINE

THE MURDER OF ASTORRE MANFREDI

After the fall of Imola and Forlì Cesare was welcomed back in Rome in a frenzy of excitement. His father Pope Alexander ordered all the clergy, all the cardinals, all officials and ambassadors to turn out to cheer his entry into the Eternal City, along with Romans who lined the streets as he passed, trumpets blaring, Cesare and his entourage of hundreds dressed in Cesarean black, others in the new attire he had adopted, the red and gold of France. He kissed his father on the feet, the hands and the mouth. Banners were raised above the Castel Sant'Angelo where he would live, and from its towers cannons fired hundreds of rounds. Rarely had the gods raised so high someone they were prepared to bring so low. He was protected by his troops, led by the likes of the Orsini, the Bentivoglii, the Baglioni, Pandolfo Petrucci, the Vitelli, Oliverotto da Ferma and others, all of whom would soon betray their glorious leader.

When Louis' French army left Rome on the 28th of June, on its way to Naples, Alexander saluted the passing troops from the heights of Castel Sant'Angelo, a proud parade of 14,000, along with 2,000 cavalry and a wagon train of 26 artillery-laden carriages, Cesare at its head, although Robert Stuart, Lord d'Aubigny, was in command. Alexander had transferred Naples from King Frederick of Naples to King Louis, a ceremony where d'Aubigny, according to Burchard, had had the privilege of being "kissed on the mouth by the cardinals."

As with all seventeen-year-olds, Astorre Manfredi had everything to live for. Of medium height, with a boyish chest and slim waist, his eyes were blue and his hair as blond as gold--curly waves of which descended to his shoulders. He was courteous, had a good word for everyone, and was as aware of his charm and sexual appeal as is every Italian boy, then as today. His family had ruled the city-state of Faenza for two centuries, and although there had been some bad apples, the Manfredi, in general, had done somewhat better than the other lords, dukes and princes of the Romagna. Although the real power behind Faenza lay with the Council that had been regent since Astorre Manfredi was named lord at age three, he had his word to say and that word was listened to more and more frequently. Faenza was one of the few veritable free spirits to exist outside Florence, and it was more of a Republic than even the Florentine city.

Indeed, Astorre had everything to live for, and perhaps even a bit more as he had received the best education available. Private tutors had instructed him in Latin, even if his daily speech was in the Italian vernacular. He had read Homer and Plato, the Greek tragedians, Suetonius and Xenophon and Plutarch, he had studied the texts of Cicero and was himself on the road to becoming an accomplished speaker.

Although puberty came later than it does today, he had already known girls and women. In fact, his extreme beauty brought blushes to the maidens in the market. His marriage to Caterina's daughter Bianca had fallen through but it was of little consequence as there were plenty of other matches to be made with girls from far more important towns than were Forlì and Imola.

Faenza was well fortified, but its strategic location meant it was in continual danger from this power or that. Like the deterrent the atomic bomb offers today, Faenza, being surrounded by powers such as Bologna, Milan, Florence and Venice, was protected because if one power dared attack, the others would tear it to pieces in order to maintain the status quo. Faenza was fortified, but with Cesare prowling around the region the citizens of the city-state decided to add to their battlements and ensure that neighboring cities would come to their succor if and when needed.

Astorre's first appeal for support went to neighboring Bologna. After all, his mother was the sister of Giovanni Bentivoglio, the lord of Bologna. Bentivoglio sent a thousand troops to Faenza but was later forced to withdraw them due to pressure from both the French King Louis XII and the pope who threatened excommunication. Louis thanked Bentivoglio for the withdrawal by taking Bologna under his wing, thus preserving the city from future ravages by Cesare. The pope also sent a note of thanks. As a sign of further capitulation, Bentivoglio agreed to feed and house a large number of Louis and Cesare's soldiers. Astorre appealed to Venice, a power he could usually depend upon, but Venice too was afraid of Louis and besides, when Louis overran Milan he had adroitly given certain lands adjoining Venice to the Serenissima, the doge now in his debt.

When Cesare did more than prowl, when he attacked and ravaged neighboring Forlì and Imola, Faenzans were armed and readied for action. At first Cesare tried charm. He met with the Council and with Astorre, informing them that the time had come for

Faenza--like Forlì and Imola--to return to the lap of the Papal States under the direction of their pope, Alexander VI. Nothing would change other than papal troops being stationed in the fort, in addition to Faenzans being enrolled in the ever-more-numerous papal armies. Astorre and the Council didn't accept Cesare's offer, as he probably knew they wouldn't, but it gave Cesare a chance to judge them both. He loved the boy as did the Faenzans, and he was known to bed lads that caught his fancy, a bent that amused his men, many of whom shared the same drift. An educated beauty would be a change from his usual bronzed and husky country fare that Cesare pushed up against a wall, at night, for fast couplings.

Cesare had far bigger fish in mind than tiny Faenza but he couldn't just bypass it. It was at the entrance to the Apennines and it controlled an important route, the Via Emilia. Anyway, if he let a little fish get away, just because he liked the ruling prince, what chance would he have with bigger states? So he attacked. To his immense surprise the Faenzans defended themselves tooth and nail, even the women took up arms. Priests melted down sacred objects to provide money, and the wealthy gave up their stocks of wheat and wine. The siege went on and on until the coming of winter, the winter of 1500, more than normally cold and snowy. Leaving enough men to make certain that Faenza wasn't supplied in food and weapons, Cesare went to spend winter in Cesena, a locality he liked so much he was thinking of making it, when all power was in his hands, the capital of the Romagna. He spent money like water, offering games, tournaments and processions, and organized huge festivities at Christmas and during Carnival. He showed his prowess by challenging the local boys to wrestling matches and horse races, all of which made him immensely popular. His admiration for the people of Faenza was such that when a merchant escaped Faenza and came to Cesena with important information concerning which parts of the walls were the less secure, Cesare had the man publicly hanged.

With the coming of spring, in March to be exact, Cesare returned to Faenza where he bombarded the walls of the city for five months, concentrating on the spot revealed by the Faenzan traitor. As food and water were lacking and the dead were piling up, as there were fewer stones and hot pitch to cast down on the invaders, Astorre and the Council were obliged to seek a truce. Cesare had no reason to give the Faenzans anything. Victory was his. But he did like the lad, and it had always been his policy to be as lenient as possible with a population. In that way he could count on the defeated to provide him with food once they had returned to the fields, as well as to give shelter for his men and horses and furnish the cannon fodder--their sons--necessary to win battles. In addition, the Council paid him personally 40,000 ducats. So, good-humoredly, he offered the boy what he wanted, and the boy wanted everything. He wanted Faenza free of foreign troops, he wanted Faenzans to be able to keep their possessions, and he wanted Cesare to forbid sacking and rape. All Astorre had to do in exchange was sign over the town to Alexander VI, which he and the Council agreed to do.

Astorre and his fifteen-year-old half-brother Gianevangelista were given their freedom, but to

Cesare's astonishment they wanted to accompany him to Rome, as today kids want to see the lights of New York. Both boys also deeply admired the most virile, courageous and experienced warrior in recent Italian history. To learn from him would make them men on the way up; Cesare was their elevator to the very top floor. It was a fatal mistake because bright lights rarely come without the accompanying greed, vice and corruption that carpet the walls in shadows.

In 1502 Astorre Manfredi's naked body came to the surface of the Tiber, caught in a fisherman's net, attached to that of his brother. Johann Burchard wrote that both boys had been participants in an orgy along with a large number of very young girls. Whether they freely consented to take part or were forced, will never be known. Whether the orgy even took place, will never be known. Cesare was said to have been involved--it would have been far from his first bacchanalia. Perhaps his father took part too. Burchard only says that ''a certain powerful person sated his lust'' on the boy. Machiavelli gets into the act because he had been there to give Cesare advice, one piece of which we find in his book: ''When a prince assumes power over a conquered territory his first obligation, if he wishes to preserve that power, is to destroy the rulers in place.'' Every time, in Italian politics, that this principle hadn't been observed, the prince lived to regret it. Turks systematically had their brothers garroted as their very first act on ascending to the throne. ''In Machiavelli's opinion Cesare, in the person of the Prince, acted prudently in having the young Manfredi executed'' (4). It's true that had Astorre lived he might have eventually become a problem for Cesare. Already immensely popular in his hometown, Astorre might have outshone Cesare himself in public adulation, an intolerable risk to a man who wore impeccable black velvet and paraded around on a white charger adorned with bells, his stirrups made of silver, his spurs of gold, but a man who was aging, a man with ''flowers''.

Burchard says that Astorre and his brother Gianevangelista had been attached together with a stone tied to their necks. The girls, all naked, had been tied together in the same fashion. The boys' bodies had torture marks.

Cesare pushed his fiendishness to extremes by greeting an envoy from Venice and springing on him the news of the murders, knowing that Venice had taken a special and highly favorable interest in both Faenza and Astorre Manfredi. The envoy was said to have not even blinked, unsurprising for a city where slaves could still be purchased, their prices varying from six ducats for a man to a hundred for a beddable girl. Burchard ends his story of Astorre by saying that, ''The young man was of such unequaled beauty and intelligence that it would be impossible to find another as sterling as he in all of Italy.'' The boy was 17. The year was 1502.

CHAPTER TEN

THE SECOND ITALIAN WAR

THE INVASION OF LOUIS XII

1499

Cesare and Alexander thought that the incursion of Louis would be a perfect time to put their house in order. Alexander's original idea was to unite the Papal States into an area equivalent in power to Naples, Venice, Florence, Bologna and Ferrara. With the aid of Louis, the reality of such an adventure was at hand, after which would come the reunification of Italy under Cesare, a perilous plan because it meant the eventual expulsion of the French. Alexander and Cesare started off small, with the seizure of lands belonging to nobles who had supported Charles, and then those they deemed their enemies, strangling some, poisoning others.

Cesare left Rome at the head of thousands of French troops and headed for the Romagna and the city-states he was set on conquering in the name of the pope because they were, after all, Papal States. On his way he visited his dear sister Lucrezia who was recuperating at Nepi after the loss of her beloved Alfonso. One wonders what they had to say to each other....

The Romagna.

A region originally held by Gauls, it was taken over by Rome, its name meaning ''land inhabited by Romans''. It was ceded to the Papal States in 1278 and held by very divisive lords, a perpetual battleground, a land of plenty and a land of massacres.

Niccolò Machiavelli explains that the Romagna was the worst nest of criminals in all of Italy. Murder, rape and theft were daily events, and the princes or lords or counts who ruled did so only to enrich themselves. The soil of the Romagna was excellent and if the lawlessness could have been brought under control, says Machiavelli, and the area united, it would have had more power than Venice or Florence or Milan or Bologna. This was the objective of Pope Alexander VI, a unified region from which his son Cesare would venture out to conquer all of Italy, a first step in uniting it into one country.

From Nepi Cesare went on to Rimini to capture the city-state from the Malatesta. On his way back he came upon the sister of the ruler of Rimini whom he had just chased from power, the grandson of Sigismondo. Cesare immediately sequestered and raped her over a period of months, denying any knowledge of her whereabouts. Anyway, he scoffed, he didn't need to rape women as they came to him willingly from everywhere. Which was true. Ambassadors from many city-states were nonetheless so upset by the abduction that they joined forces in demanding that Alexander severely punish his son. Alexander too was reported as being upset, but in the end, what could he do? The woman was eventually restored to her husband but from what she reported later, either she was suffering from Stockholm syndrome or her months with Cesare hadn't been all that traumatizing, because she refused to accuse him of any wrongdoing.

The time had come for Lucrezia to marry again, a marriage which would, naturally, benefit the pope. Alexander thusly chose the son of Duke Ercole of Ferrara [Ercole I d'Este], another Alfonso, Alfonso I d'Este, for his daughter Lucrezia. Behind closed doors the Duke of Ferrara laughed at such pretention. His family was noble, old and wealthy, that of Alexander hick parvenus. Ercole had heard stories about them all, that Alexander had prostitutes from the best bordellos brought to him after dinner, that Cesare slept during the day and whored at night, that both he and his dad had shared Lucrezia, that they were murderous slime, socially nonexistent and morally rotten to the core.

Yet … his own boy was perhaps no better. Alfonso was known to have two interests in life, making cannons in his own personal foundry and parading around town at night, his sword in one hand, his erect cock in the other. His former wife had been so fed up with him that she turned to women for satisfaction. But the wedding did take place since Louis XII of France wanted it, all because he needed the Borgia to further his ambitions. The price Ercole demanded would have been dismissed out of hand by any other person in Italy, but not Alexander who disposed of literally bottomless resources, resources brought in, in multiple ways, every single day, via every church in the country. Alfonse was 26, Lucrezia still only 21. Parties were thrown in Rome prior to her leaving the city, one of which, in 1501, was the famous Banquet of the

Chestnuts, at the end of which candelabra were taken from the tables and placed on the floor, and chestnuts were strewn around, which naked courtesans picked up, creeping on hands and knees between the chandeliers. Prizes were announced for those who could perform sexually most often with the courtesans, such as tunics of silk and shoes. William Manchester in his *A World Lit Only by Fire*, wrote: ''Servants kept score of each man's orgasms, for the pope greatly admired virility and measured a man's machismo by his ejaculative capacity.... After everyone was exhausted, His Holiness distributed prizes....''

The trip to Ferrara and the celebration there cost a fortune, but the wedding night came off well. Alexander was told that Alfonso had contented Lucrezia that night and then took his pleasure with other women during the day. The pope supposedly thought this just fine as Alfonso was a young man and, as such, multiple adventures were good for him. The historian Johann Burchard--not only present at Alexander's court but was Alexander's Master of Ceremonies, the man who organized court celebrations and festivities--wrote that all the talk of lubricity inspired the pope to increase the number of prostitutes he welcomed into his rooms that night: ''His Holiness has taken on a new lease of life in consequence of the news from Ferrara and every night he is commanding into his presence young women chosen from the best Roman brothels.'' As always in Italy, love was in the air. [It was also Burchard who related the Banquet of the Chestnuts.]

The marriage between Alfonso and Lucrecia was sexually open from the beginning, both available to outsiders. Yet Alfonso had his limits, possibly through jealousy that she was enjoying more nocturnal visitors than he, because he had a priest murdered and a poet, Ercole Strozzi, lacerated with ''twenty-two stab wounds and his throat cut'' (2), both having served as intermediaries between Lucrezia and her lovers.

Because Lucrezia will now leave these pages, I'll reveal here her final years: While Caterina Sforza ended her life by entering a nunnery where she married Christ, Lucrezia, despite ever-increasing amounts of donations to convents and churches as she grew older, never abandoned that part of herself that wanted to be a woman to men of flesh and blood. Right up to the end she continued affairs with men, the two most important being Francesco Gonzaga of Mantua and poet Pietro Bembo, for whom she wrote letters of stupefying sensuality [for the period]. Right up to the finish line she continued to give Alfonso children, five in all. At age thirty-nine, just a few months after the death of her mother Vannozza, she died giving birth, birth to a child and birth to a star, her star, that shines as brightly now as it did half a millennium ago, solid proof that it is better to use life and be used by it than to flee the storm, dodging the droplets, seeking an illusive shelter that exists, in the end, for none of us.

Alexander sent Cesare to conquer Forlì and Imola, ruled by Caterina Riario Sforza de' Medici, and Faenza headed by Astorre Manfredi. For Cesare, Caterina of Forlì and Imola, and Astorre of Faenza, were an interlude to much bigger acts of bravura. He went on to take Urbino, the citadel of the Montefeltro, and a dozen other city-states. Along the way he heard stories about some of his captains, traitors in the pay of Roman nobles eager for the reign of Alexander to come to an end by assassinating their leader, Cesare.

He moved on to Siena, sacking, destroying, maiming, killing and raping. Those who wouldn't give up their money were tortured; if they were found to have nothing to give up, their throats were slashed [the soldiers were instructed that this was the best way not to blunt a sharp sword or dagger].

The French army of 14,000, accompanied by Cesare and led by d'Aubigny, a Scotsman by birth, made its way to Naples with, Burchard tells us, a very inadequate number of prostitutes: 16. On the way only Capua put up a fight, but the town was betrayed from someone inside. This person, as well as the entire population, women, children, priests and nuns, were slaughtered in the usual manner Louis XII had developed as a warning to the towns to come, slaughtered after serving the men's sexual needs. When the troops entered Naples, there was no confrontation. Cesare, age 26, was rewarded 40,000 ducats for his aid. The year was 1501.

The ruler of Urbano, Guidobaldo da Montefeltro, had come from extremely hallowed lineage. His father had been none other than the most famous condottiere of perhaps all time, Federico da Montefeltro. Federico was a Renaissance man, the possessor of a truly wonderful library and study done in *trompe-l'oeil*. He's thought to have taken power by killing his stepbrother Oddantonio, as stated earlier, made easy by the population of Urbino who were unhappy with his reign. He inspired loyalty among his men, sharing his gains as condottiere with them. Because his fees were high, he was able to enrich Urbino. He had surgeons remove part of his nose so that he could see with the eye remaining him, the other having been lost in a tournament. He fought for Florence, for Milan, for Naples and then against Florence before the Treaty of Lodi brought peace to the three city-states. This was the reason why Renaissance battles were rarely murderous. A condottiere knew that the lord he fought against today might become the lord who paid him gold to fight at his side tomorrow.

Guidobaldo fled when he heard that Cesare was near, although Alexander had sent a messenger offering him the red hat of a cardinal if he would agree to give up power peacefully. He turned down the offer, a move that displeased Alexander to the extent that he circulated the rumor that Guidobaldo was impotent, certainly true as his wife came out with a statement saying that she would prefer him as a brother to not having him as a husband. Guidobaldo had fought for Alexander against Charles VIII, but as usual when Alexander no longer needed someone, he was cast aside. Guidobaldo would get his revenge, though. After the death of Alexander he would return to govern Urbino and help Julius II in regaining the Romagna for the church. He would be succeeded by a della Rovere, his sister's child and a nephew of Julius II. Like that of his famous father, the court of Urbino was and would continue as the most refined in Italy. Cesare entered Urbino unopposed and stole what he could, sending the major paintings and sculptures to Rome. One piece was Michelangelo's *Cupid*. Experts had declared that it was not only Greek, but that it was an example of Greek mastery in sculpture, never equaled since. Michelangelo then admitted that it was his, and that he had buried it as a stunt to get attention. It worked. He was called to Rome by Cardinal Raffaele Riario who was a renowned collector of art. The rest, as one says, is history.

Like Charles VIII and Louis XII, Machiavelli too was smitten by Cesare, who became his model as the perfect tyrant. He wrote that the man never rested, which allowed him to move from one place to another, taking an adversary by surprise. Cesare would often summon him in the middle of the night or early morning, his syphilitic face covered in gauze.

The copyright for the scene of the mafia sitting around a banquet table, offered rich gifts to ease them into a spirit of tranquility and insouciance, prior to their being slaughtered, goes to Cesare Borgia and dates from 1503. Cesare surrounded himself with some of Italy's greatest tyrants and cutthroats. There was Vitellozzo Vitelli, lord of several minor towns, but known as a condottiere at the head of his own army that he placed under the highest bidder. He and his brother Paolo had fought for Florence until Paolo was put to death for supposed treachery. Vitelli then fought for Cesare, a man he respected so much he conquered the town of Senigallia as a gift to the charismatic Borgia, a gift he had to relinquish to Florence, following orders from Cesare who was himself following orders from King Louis XII under whom Cesare had placed himself. Embittered, Vitelli met with other unhappy condottieri at Magione to plot Cesare's downfall.

Oliverotto da Fermo, like Vitelli, was set on following Cesare to the ends of the earth, even capturing Camerino for him. Camerino was a small fief ruled by the da Varani since 1262. The lords now were Giulio Cesare da Varano and his three sons, all of whom Oliverotto had strangled in their castle La Pergola. Pope Alexander VI then visited the town alongside his son Cesare and installed, as Duke of Camerino, his daughter Lucrezia's four-year-old son Giovanni, the child she had had with the servant Pedro Calderon, the boy Cesare had murdered in the Vatican as he sought shelter in the robes of Alexander, knifing him with such fury that the boy's blood splattered the pope's face. Instead of thanking Oliverotto sufficiently for Camerino, Cesare neglected him in favor of greater men, the first of which was King Louis, leaving Oliverotto stranded along the road like an abandoned dog.

The Orsini brothers were also present at Magione, Paolo, Roberto and Francesco. A fourth brother, Cardinal Giambattista Orsini, the supposed brains behind the plot to destroy Cesare, was held back in Rome. Pandolfo Petrucci attended the meeting at Magione. He had gained power in Siena thanks to wealth inherited from his brother and the fortune held by his father-in-law. Petrucci used his money to put his supporters in positions of power, earning enemies, among whom was his father-in-law who plotted to have him assassinated. Petrucci struck first, murdering him in 1500. Petrucci managed Siena so deftly--avoiding wars and bringing financial stability--that he won what was literally the love of the Sienese. Convinced that he would make a far more just and competent leader than

Cesare, he joined the others in the revolt, but fearing a trap at Senigallia, where Cesare would later convoke them all, he alleged other business to stay away. Petrucci was thought to have been behind the death of Pius III who was pope for 26 days, by poisoning, in order to make way for Julius II.

The Bentivoglio family had held Bologna since the early 1300s, a town with an extremely important university that had carried out medical dissections in public for centuries, a city-state made powerful largely thanks to marriage-alliances with the Sforza, Visconti and the Gonzaga of Mantua. The leader now, Giovanni Bentivoglio, had done whatever he could to gain the favor of King Louis XII and Cesare, even withdrawing the troops he had promised in support of Faenza, ruled by his daughter's son, Astorre Manfredi. He surrendered fortifications to Cesare and put food and lodging at the disposition of a part of his troops. But then Louis withdrew his support, saying he couldn't stand in the way of Pope Alexander VI who had final supremacy over Bologna. Afraid that Cesare would take possession of the city, Giovanni sent his son Ermes to Magione to join the other conspirators. The young Ermes proclaimed, in front of the participants, that he himself would kill Cesare.

The catalyst for the meeting of these gentlemen in Magione was a rumor, that King Louis XII of France feared that Alexander VI sought the union of all of Italy under his son Cesare Borgia. This meant that both Spain, which occupied Naples, and France, which occupied Milan, would be escorted *manu militari* out of the country. The men at Magione felt that Cesare had been loyally served, and had given nothing back in exchange. Worse, he had deprived most of the men of their conquests, if in doing so he could further his own ambitions and/or ingratiate himself to the all-powerful French king. Others, like the Bentivoglii, just wanted to keep that which had been theirs for generations, more and more difficult with the fearless, pitiless and ambitious son of the pope roaming about. Some of the complotters, those who believed the rumor, even envisioned the possibility that Louis would take Cesare back to France with him and imprison him for life, as the French had done to Ludovico Sforza when they seized Milan.

So at Magione they all came together, even Vitelli, so stricken by syphilis that he couldn't even walk and had to be toted around on a stretcher. Another potential plotter, Gianpaolo Baglioni, stayed away, warning that they all risked being ''devoured one by one by the dragon'' (2). Had they stuck together they would easily have won. Cesare had surrendered the mass of his troops to Louis for his move against Naples, leaving him with but a handful. The complotters, on the other hand, had over 10,000. They all then headed for Senigallia where Cesare had demanded their presence.

Not all of the traitors would be able to make it to Senigallia, but those who did came with their own troops. As their leader, Cesare told them that his soldiers had priority in lodging. Troops other than his own were to evacuate Senigallia and find quarters outside the town limits. These, Cesare had quietly surrounded by his men.

They all entered the castle of Senigallia where a banquet in Cesare's honor was spread out. At a certain moment Cesare excused himself to answer a call of nature. Those present, Vitelli and the Orsini brothers, Francesco and Paolo, and Paolo's son Fabio, and Oliverotto, were immediately set upon by Micheletto de Corella and his men and tied up. The Orsini were put aside until Cardinal Orsini in Rome and his brother Giulio Orsini could be stopped by Alexander. Oliverotto and Vitelli were tried during the night. They begged for their lives but when found guilty were seated back-to-back and strangled with a violin string. When word that the Orsini in Rome had been arrested, the Orsini at Senigallia were murdered. The Orsini in Rome were poisoned, although the cardinal's death was described as being by natural causes. When Julius II took power a priest came forward and confessed to the poisoning, under orders from Alexander. The man, Asquino de Colloredo, spoke of the infallible white powder the Borgia used in all of their masked assassinations.

So ended what is known in history as the Revolt of the Condottieri.

Cesare Borgia.

''Dagger in hand, it was said, Cesare chased Perotto [Pedro Calderon's pet name] through the anterooms of the pope. Stumbling into the aged Alexander, Perotto was caught by Cesare, who plunged his dagger repeatedly into the wretched, quivering body. Perotto's blood spurted upwards, drenching Alexander's face and the papal robes he wore'', a quote from Marion Johnson's *The Borgias*, 1981.

In order to continue his conquests Cesare needed ever more money. Alexander helped out where he could by emptying the palaces of the condottieri mutineers. In addition, new cardinals were nominated, raising 180,000 ducats. Cardinal Gianbattista Ferrari became fatally ill owing to, according to rumor, the Borgia white powder. Alexander had his residence emptied of its gold and jewels, bringing him 80,000 ducats, not counting his clothes and jewels. Ferrari had been hated as he had helped no one but himself. He was so avaricious, went a story, that he refused to pay St. Peter 1,000 ducats as entry into Heaven. He refused, too, to pay the lesser fee of 500. He even refused the 1 ducat that St. Peter requested, after which the furious saint said, ''Then go to Hell!,'' which was, apparently, exactly what Ferrari had deserved all along.

Cardinal Giovanni Michiel died after ''a strange session of vomiting,'' wrote Venetian ambassador Antonio Giustinian. ''As soon as the Pope heard of his death he sent a man to his house and, before dawn, it was completely plundered, the death bringing the Pope over 150,000 ducats'' (2).

As mentioned above, Alexander named nine new cardinals, three Italians, one German and five

Spaniards, but no French, each paying 20,000 ducats for the honor. One man, disappointed at not being made a cardinal, Francesco Troche, badmouthed Alexander and Cesare. Fearing that Cesare would kill him, he fled to Corsica where Cesare's men captured him. Brought back to Rome, he was strangled by Micheletto. [Another version has him committing suicide by jumping ship on the way to the mainland.] Cesare's enemy Jacopo di Santacroce was hanged that same day, as a warning that death was the response to those who maligned him and his father.

CHAPTER ELEVEN

THE DEATH OF POPE ALEXANDER VI

THE FINAL BATTLE OF CESARE BORGIA

Cesare was no fool. He knew his father would not live on forever. He had thusly looted Italy of every ducat seizable, he had storerooms of weapons at his disposal and his troops loved this handsome fearless man who conceded their every wish as long as they remained loyal to him. What he hadn't counted on was *his* nearly dying at exactly the same time as his father, which is precisely what happened. What he hadn't counted on either was the election of a new pope even more vigorous, intelligent and belligerent than Alexander VI.

Cesare and his father had been invited to a banquet after which they both fell seriously ill.

Illness was nothing new to the Renaissance. All the actors in this book, all without exception, had fallen ill multiple times throughout their lives. Lucrezia, for example, was continuously sick--especially following her many miscarriages. Illness came from literally everywhere, bad food, incredibly diseased water that one drank or swam in; illness came from common flue, from typhus, cholera and malaria; from flees and rats and dogs and other people. It came through breathing, sweating, defecating and fucking. Illness favored the months of July and August, hot muggy months propitious to dysentery. All of Alexander's predecessors, Innocent, Sixtus, Pius and Calixtus had died during those months. And it was now July, "the month," Alexander had said, "when fat men croak," and both he and Cesare were at death's door. Perhaps they believed, as did the people, that they had been poisoned during the banquet. Perhaps, as some said, they themselves had tried to poison their host, an ever-criticizing cardinal they both could well do without-- and his money they could well do with, but somehow they had drunk their own means of murder. As Alexander was now seventy-three, he was in more danger than his young son. They were both bled although, unlike his father, Cesare was plunged into cold water, the accepted cure for fever. [Chronicler Bernardino Zambotti stated that if Cesare survived, "it was chiefly due to the fact that he was placed inside the still warm entrails of two mules" (2).] Alexander received last rites but not Cesare, a former cardinal, who vaunted his atheism.

Cesare had been accused of heinous crimes, of murder, including his own brother, assassinations, poisonings, rapes and incest with his sister, even the buggering of Astorre Manfredi and his fifteen-year-old brother before ordering them strangled and thrown into the Tiber. Now he directed Micheletto de Corella to loot the pope's rooms and, putting a knife to the throat of its guardian, Cardinal Casanova, Micheletto made him disclose the places Alexander had hidden, *à la Volpone*, his gold and jewels, worth, wrote the Venetian ambassador Giustinian, 500,000 ducats. In his haste he overlooked rings and a tiara that servants later found and stole, along with his clothes, furniture, bedding, drapes and tapestries. When the cardinals made an inventory later still, they came up with a further 25,000 ducats in gems and gold, said Burchard. Burchard, as Master of Ceremonies, was responsible for the pope's burial, and reported that the pope's rings had been wrenched from his fingers. Alexander's body was placed in the usual papal triple coffin. As customary, paid paupers carried his remains, swollen and black, wrote Burchard, to St. Peter's where the body was abandoned--no one even saw, apparently, to lighting a vigil of candles. He stank intolerably and, Burchard concludes, he was erect there where he had been erect all his life.

Later, fearful that the "angry people might not climb up to reach the body and someone who had been wronged by the Pope would get his revenge, the bier was moved behind an iron grille and there the body remained throughout the day, with the iron grille firmly closed," wrote the bishop of Sessa (2). The Orsini took advantage of the death of Spanish Alexander by setting fire to every home and business belonging to Rome's Spaniards.

Overnight Cesare lost it all. His palaces were sacked and the lands he had conquered were recovered by the counts, lords, dukes and princes he had overturned. He was carried away by litter to recuperate at his sister's retreat of Nepi, where he found his mother Vannozza and his brother Jofrè. Della Rovere made his way through the streets of Rome to the conclave, surrounded by his own army of crossbowmen, unaware of the presence of Micheletto that Cesare had sent at the head of a hit team to kill him, one of many failed attempts at ending Rovere's life (1). The Venetian ambassador Giustinian was dispatched to ask Cesare to remove his men from Castel Sant'Angelo which had been taken by Micheletto de Corella's troops. In return, Cesare was promised to be confirmed in all of his functions. The conclave elected Pius III, a good man who had been archbishop of Siena. Among the cardinals was Ippolito d'Este. Ippolito had fallen in love with a local beauty, a girl who claimed that she far preferred another of Ippolito's brothers, Giulio, whose beautiful brown eyes alone were worth more than all of Ippolito. In response the cardinal waylaid his brother and tried to cut out those wonderful eyes. Another brother, Alfonso, convinced Ippolito to ask for pardon, but this was not sufficient enough for Giulio who suffered horrible pain and the near total loss of sight. He decided to get revenge on both brothers, Alfonso and Ippolito, by having them killed. He united his forces with still another of his brothers, Ferrante. Their conspiracy was discovered, however, and although Alfonso would not have them executed, he did send them to prison. Ferrante died in his dungeon forty-three years later,

Giulio endured for fifty-three. In Rome Ippolito got revenge on the intolerably arrogant Cesare by bedding Cesare's favorite mistress, left alone while he was at Nepi, as well as bedding Sancia (3). No one trusted Cesare, and no one wanted him back in Rome, but Pius III swallowed Cesare's assurances that he wished to return simply to die in the holy city. He was nevertheless still so ill that after his return to Rome he had to stay in bed for several weeks, during which he lost his hold over his own troops.

Julius, as Machiavelli had foreseen, kept none of his promises. A wagon train of Cesare's wealth was stopped and seized in Bologna, and turned back under papal escort to Rome. His money in Genoa was blocked while Julius did the paperwork to retrieve it from the banks there. Micheletto was arrested outside Ferrara at the head of a pack of mules carrying the gold and jewels Cesare had stolen from the Vatican and were now destined for safe keeping by his sister Lucrezia. Cesare offered 10,000 gold ducats for Micheletto's release, which was refused. Micheletto was turned over to Julius in Rome who had him sent to Castel Sant'Angelo and tortured in order to find out where Cesare kept his treasure. Although he refused, he was later set free. Machiavelli found him employment in Florence, but it was in Milan that he was murdered, under unknown circumstances.

Florence refused safe passage so that Cesare could go north to France where his young wife awaited him, and where he could find safety under Louis XII. Then Julius issued a warrant for his arrest, accusing him of the murders of his brother Juan, his sister's husband

Alfonso, Astorre Manfredi and Astorre's brother, as well as Vitelli and Oliverotto garroted in Senigallia, the two Orsini strangled, the Orsini cardinal poisoned in Rome, Varano and his sons, and others. But in exchange for his giving up the wealth he had hoarded, and the fortifications in the Romagna still in possession of those who remained loyal to him, Cesare was allowed exile in Spain.

He retired to Chinchilla, a mountain castle in the heights near Valencia. Machiavelli blamed all of Cesare's disasters on his original agreement to back Julius' bid for the papacy, after Julius had promised him that he could retain his papal functions, his army and the Romagna. Machiavelli could not understand how someone so intelligent could have done something so stupid. Others around Cesare suggested that his illness had adversely affected his brain.

In the mountain retreat of Chinchilla things went wrong for Cesare when his exile turned into captivity. Isabella of Spain decided to follow Julius' lead in prosecuting him for the deaths of his brother Juan, duke of Gadía, and Lucrezia's husband, Alfonso of Aragon, both of Spanish lineage. He escaped from his castle by climbing down a rope. He made his way by boat and trek to Pamplona in Navarre, a place he knew well as he had been named bishop of Pamplona at age 16. He was well received within the fortress of his brother-in-law Juan of Navarre who put him at the head of his troops. As the city-states in Spain were in perpetual upheaval just like their Italian counterparts, Cesare was constantly at war. His last day found him chasing a band of rebels. At age thirty-two he was still in the full glory of his bravado and virility and so thought nothing of outdistancing his men. Alas, the rebels he was chasing turned to face him and, highly outnumbered, he received many blows, one of which was the fatal plunge of a dagger to his throat, just above the armor. He fell into a ravine, dead. Juan of Navarre had the body buried in the small church of Viana where it lies to this day. The year was 1507.

Cesare was a man of his times, violent and choleric, imminently Italian is his duplicity, deceit and cunning, whose charisma was such that his legend and bravura have spanned 500 years.

CHAPTER TWELVE

AFTERMATH

Julius II was different from the other popes, with the exception of Alexander VI, in having balls, big brass balls like those of Leonidas, whose statue, on a high pedestal, is in the midst of the town of Sparta, should you ever get that way (12).

Guicciardini had this to say about Julius: ''He was a soldier in a cassock; he drank and swore heavily as he led his troops; he was willful, coarse, bad-tempered and difficult to manage. He would ride his horse up the Lateran stairs to his papal bedroom and tether it at the door.'' And he loved being called the Warrior Pope.

Born Giuliano della Rovere, he may have been both the son *and* lover of Sixtus IV, an accusation made also against Alexander VI and *his* bastard son Cesare [several sources, existent at the time, maintain that this was so, but then Julius and Sixtus, Alexander and Cesare, had many enemies]. He was educated among

Franciscans by Sixtus himself, and was Sixtus' altar boy when Sixtus became pope. Della Rovere was endowed by the same Sixtus with numerous bishoprics, making him a wealthy young man. He was a papal legate in France for four years, which served him mightily when Alexander became pope and he had to flee to France to escape Alexander's wrath because he had accused him of buying the papal election. He convinced the French king Charles VIII to intervene in Italian affairs by invading Italy, but Alexander, subtle, intelligent and *in power*, outmatched della Rovere who had to wait for Alexander's death to have a try at the Vatican, but another was elected, Pope Pius III, who luckily for Julius had only 26 days to live. In the meantime della Rovere gained Cesare's support due to Cesare's illness which nearly finished him off, and due to della Rovere's promise to reinstate Cesare as head of papal troops and assure him that he would retain all of the land he had conquered under his father Alexander. Cesare was no fool except this one time. He gave his support to della Rovere who was unanimously elected pope except for two votes, della Rovere's own and the French Cardinal d'Amboise who wanted the job for the glory of France [receiving della Rovere's vote, out of friendship]. Naturally, the usual bribes--money and a mightier position on the food chain--won the day. Cesare was killed and Julius II erased every remaining trace of Alexander. Nigel Cawthorne quotes Julius in his *Sex Lives of the Popes*, ''I will not live in the same rooms as the Borgia. Alexander desecrated the Holy Church as none before. He usurped the papal power by the devil's aid, and I forbid under the pain of excommunication anyone to speak or think of Borgia again. His name and memory must be forgotten. It must be crossed out of every document and memorial. His reign must be obliterated. All paintings made of the Borgia or for them must be covered over with black crepe. All the tombs of the Borgia must be opened and their bodies sent back to where they belong--to Spain."

Giuliano della Rovere, the future Julius II, left, with Sixtus IV, his purported father, seated.

One of the major problems for the new pope was Henry VIII who wanted a divorce. Julius granted a papal dispensation that allowed Henry to marry Catherine of Aragon who had been Henry's brother's bride for six months before he died, leaving Catherine a virgin as he had been too ill to be operative--although the day after the wedding he bragged to his friends, "Last night I visited the depths of Spain." The refusal to allow the divorce by Julius' successor Clement VII would end Catholicism in England, all because the king wanted to reign supreme and fuck his way through five additional wives.

The second problem was the Papal States, governed by lords, dukes, princes and counts that the pope wanted returned to the bosom of the church [as had Alexander VI]. In a series of wars far too complicated and ephemeral to discuss here--the War of the Holy League, the Battle of Agnadello, the War of the League of Cambrai, among others--he simply died too soon to succeed, of fever, and with him his dream of a united Italy died too.

Julius had put Michelangelo to the task of constructing his tomb, commissioned in 1505 and finished in 1545. It was originally intended for St. Peter's Basilica but wound up in the church of San Pietro in Vincoli. Although the actual tomb is colossal, with 7 statues, including the magnificent Moses, the original would have been far bigger, comprising 40 statues, some of the unfinished ones now on view in the Louvre. Only the Moses has a commanding presence and an anecdote has it that it was so lifelike that when finished Michelangelo struck it on the knee with a hammer, saying ''NOW SPEAK!'' The hammer mark can be seen today [that tourist guides love to point out to visitors].

Michelangelo's *Moses*

Michelangelo had also been appointed to paint the Sistine Chapel, named after Sixtus IV who restored it. Julius was said to have appreciated the physical beauty of the men painted by Michelangelo but part of their beauty was destroyed forever when one of Michelangelo's associates, Daniele da Volterra, was ordered to cover up the genitals following the genius's death. But he didn't touch the acorns and oak leaves present, the first representing the male glans and the second the renewal of sexuality, among other things. The central *Creation of Adam* is certainly the most stirring work of art known to humanity.

One of Julius' lovers is thought to have been Giovanni Alidosi who accompanied della Rovere to France. Julius made him a cardinal and he served as an intermediary between the pope and Michelangelo, as both were headstrong and difficult [just the negotiations concerning the Sistine Chapel, before a single brush stroke, took two years]. In fighting to recapture the Papal States, Julius lost a battle with

Bologna, the governess of which was Alidosi's responsibility. In consequence Alidosi had three pawns found guilty of aiding the Bolognese. They were strangled under his orders. Of Alidosi, Cardinal Bembo said, ''Faith meant nothing to him, nor religion, nor trustworthiness, nor shame, nor anything that was holy.'' Much hated, Alidosi was often caught and tried by various rulers, notably those of Bologna and Urbino, ruled by the pope's nephew, Francesco Maria della Rovere, but instead of executing the reviled cardinal he was always given a trial, time enough for Julius to intervene in his favor. As Francesco had been appointed general to conquer Bologna and had failed to do so, he was summoned to Rome to explain himself to his uncle the pope. After the meeting, while heading back to his lodgings on horseback, accompanied by a group of his soldiers, he crossed the path of Alidosi who was on his way to dine with the pope. Alidosi saluted Francesco in an arrogant way that displeased one of Francesco's followers, just a youngster, who dismounted and knifed Alidosi, sitting on his mule, in the throat. From then on it was an eating-frenzy of boys out to kill each other. Francesco's soldiers won out, and while Alidosi's men went scurrying away, Francesco's took turns slicing off pieces of Alidosi's face and plunging daggers into his body. Julius had the pieces interred and realpolitik obliging, suffered his pain in private.

Another lover was supposedly Luigi Pulci, a poet described by Cellini as being beautiful and talented. The Venetian diarist Girolamo Priuli maintains that Julius brought to Rome ''some very handsome young men with whom he was publicly rumored to have sex, and he was said to be the passive partner." When attacking Bologna a sonnet circulated, advising Julius to return to Rome where he could content himself with "Squarcia and Curzio in your holy palace / keeping the bottle in your mouth and a cock up your ass." It *was* true that he drank a lot. [The full life of the pope can be found in my book *Julius II*.]

In 1506 Julius made plans to demolish the old church of St. Peter's and replace it with a huge basilica, the whole serving to house Julius' final resting place, the greatest tomb ever erected. Michelangelo was chosen to design it as well as to help with the basilica, but over the next 120 years the combined efforts of popes and architects were needed to see it through. It is believed that St. Peter was crucified there, at the emplacement of the current obelisk, by Nero who held the Christians responsible for the burning of the city. As for Julius, Michelangelo finally finished his tomb after 40 years of bargaining and labor. Julius wasn't interred there though. For all his efforts he was accorded a simple slab of marble on the floor of the basilica, that people walk over every day, little aware of the headstrong warrior beneath.

NOTE

I hope the reader will forgive me for the constant references to Showtime's *The Borgias*. I did so because the series is simply too exquisite for words, in its reconstruction of palaces and fortifications, interior decors and clothing, the actors of often sublime beauty, boys and girls alike, and the scenes of same-sex love between Micheletto and his virile lover are truly extraordinary. The series brought life to Ferrante and his museum, and brilliantly told the story of Caterina Sforza, sorely neglected by historians. DVDs of the series are on the market, three parts in what should have been a four-part collection, but the fourth segment had to be scrubbed due to the incredible cost of the production, the expenditures clearly visible on the screen, as well as the salaries of what the world has best in actors.

POSTSCRIPT

The only truth about the Borgia is that we will
never know the truth.
mbhone@gmail.com

APPENDIX

CHRONOLOGY

1378
Birth of Alonso de Borja.
1416
Alfonso V becomes King of Aragon and Alonso de Borja enters his service in 1417.
1431
The birth of Rodrigo Borgia, future Alexander VI.
1442
Alfonso becomes Alfonso I of Naples (1442-1458).
1456
Rodrigo Borgia is made a cardinal and his brother Pier Luigi Borgia is named captain-general of the papal army.

1457
Rodrigo Borgia is made vice-chancellor.
1458
Calixtus III dies, succeeded by Pius II.
Ferrante (Ferdinand I) becomes King of Naples.
Death of Pier Luigi Borgia.
1460
Rodrigo told by Pius II to stop his orgies.
1466
Galeazzo Maria Sforza becomes Duke of Milan (1466-1476)
He commissions da Vinci's *The Last Supper*.
1471
Francesco della Rovere elected Pope Sixtus IV.
Six of his nephews-cum-lovers-cum-sons named cardinals.
1475
Birth of Cesare.
1476
Birth of Juan Borgia.
1478
The Pazzi and Girolamo Riario try to kill Lorenzo *Il Magnifico* de' Medici
1480
Birth of Lucrezia Borgia.
1488
Murder of Girolamo Riario, Caterina Sforza's husband.
1489
Ludovico Sforza becomes Duke of Milan (1489-1500).
1492
Rodrigo Borgia becomes Alexander VI.
Death of Lorenzo *Il Magnifico* de' Medici.

1493
Lucrezia maries Giovanni Sforza / Jofrè marries Sancia of Aragon / Juan marries Maria Enriquez de Luna of Spain.

Alexander divides the world between the Spanish and the Portuguese.

1494
Death of Ferrante of Naples; his son Alfonso II takes his place.

Charles VIII invades Italy in hopes of taking Naples. The beginning of the Renaissance Wars.

1495
Alfonso II abdicates in favor of his son Ferdinand II.

Charles VIII meets Alexander in Rome.

Following the Battle of Fornovo, Charles VIII withdraws to France.

1496
Frederick IV becomes King of Naples.

1497
Juan Borgia murdered, certainly by Cesare.

Lucrezia divorces Giovanni Sforza.

1498
Lucrezia's lover Pedro Calderon murdered by Cesare.

Charles VIII hits his head against a doorframe and dies.

Lucrezia marries Alfonso of Aragon, Sancia's brother.

Savonarola burned at the stake.

1499
Alexander excommunicates Romagna lords in preparation for Cesare's conquests.

1500
Cesare takes Forlì and Imola and captures Caterina Sforza.

Lucrezia's beloved Alfonso strangled under orders from Cesare.

Louis XII invades and takes Milan.

1501

Lucrezia married Alfonso d'Este, both unfaithful.

Louis XII takes Naples (as King Louis III 1501-1504).

1502

Cesare puts an end to the Revolt of the Condottieri.

Death of Astorre Manfredi, killed by Cesare after an orgy.

Cesare meets Louis XII in Milan

Machiavelli meets Cesare, the hero of his *The Prince*.

1503

Revolt against Cesare.

Spain captures Naples.

Alexander VI dies / Cesare deathly ill.

Pius III is elected pope, dies and is followed by Julius II in the shortest conclave in history.

1504

Cesare goes to Spain and is imprisoned.

Isabella of Spain dies.

Michelangelo finishes his *David*.

1505

Alfonso I d'Este Duke of Ferrara (1505-1534) becomes the husband of Lucrezia Borgia.

1506

Cesare escapes prison and flees to Navarre.

Sancia dies.

1507

Cesare dies in battle.

1508

Micheletto da Corella dies.

1509

Caterina Riario Sforza de' Medici dies in a convent.
1513
Julius II dies.
1514
Leonardo finishes his chef-d'oeuvre *John the Baptist*.
1519
Da Vinci dies.
Lucrezia dies in childbirth, months after her mother's death.

SOURCES

(1) See my book *Julius II*.
(2) From Christopher Hibbert's essential *The Borgia*, 2008.
(3) From G.J. Meyer's excellent book *The Borgia*, 2013.
(4) From E.R. Chamberlin's *The Fall of the House of Borgia*.
(5) See my book *A History of Florentine Homosexuality*.
(6) See my book *Cellini*.
(7) From Marion Johnson's *The Borgia*, 1981.
(8) See my book *Julius II*.
(10) See my book *Renaissance Homosexuality*.
(11) From Gerard Noel's *Renaissance Popes*, 2006.
(12) See my book *SPARTA*.

Abbott Jacob, *History of Pyrrhus*, 2009.
Ady, Cecilia, *A History of Milan under the Sforza*, 1907.
Aggleton, Peter, *Men Who Sell Sex*, 1999.
Aldrich, *Who's Who in Gay and Lesbian History*, 2001.
Aldrich, Robert, *The Seduction of the Mediterranean*.
Andress, David, *The Terror*, 2005.
Aronson, Marc, *Sir Walter Ralegh*, 2000.
Baglione, *Caravaggio*, circa 1600.
Baker Simon, *Ancient Rome*, 2006.

Barber, Richard, *The Devil's Crown*, 1978.
Barber, Stanley, *Alexandros*, 2010.
Bellori, *Caravaggio*, circa 1600.
Bicheno, Hugh, *Vendetta*, 2007.
Boswell, John, *Christianity and Homosexuality*, 1980.
Boswell, John, *Same-Sex Unions*, 1994.
Boyd, Douglas, *April Queen*, 2004.
Boyles, David, *Blondel's Song*, 2005.
Bramly, Serge, *Leonardo*, 1988. A wonderful book.
Bret, Davis, *Trailblazers*, 2009.
Bull, Lew, *Memoirs of a Hustler*, 2010.
Burg, B.R., *Gay Warriors*, 2002.
Bury and Meiggs, *A History of Greece*, 1975.
Calimach, Andrew, *Lover's Legends*, 2002.
Carpenter, Edward, *The Intermediate Sex*, 1912.
Carroll, Stuart, *Maryrs & Murderers*, 2009.
Cavel Benjamin, *Rumble, Young Man, Rumble*, 2003.
Cawthorne, Nigel, *Sex Lives of the Popes*, 1996
Cellini, Benvenuto, *Autobiography of Benvenuto Cellini*.
Ceram, C.W., *Gods, Graves and Scholars*, 1951.
Chamberlin, E.R. *The Fall of the House of Borgia*, 1974
Clark, Christopher, *Iron Kingdom*, 2006.
Clark, Gerald, *Capote*, 1988.
Clerc, Thomas, *Maurice Sachs, Le Désoeuvré*, 2005.
Cloulas Ivan, *The Borgia*, 1989.
Cloulas, Ivan, *Jules II*, 1990.
Cooper, John, *The Queen's Agent*, 2011.
Cowan, Thomas, *Gay Men and Women*, 1988.
Crompton, Louis, *Byron and Greek Love*, 1985.
Crompton, Louis, *Homosexuality and Civilization*, 2003.
Crowley, Roger, *Empires of the Sea*, 2008. Marvelous.
Davidson, James, *Courtesans and Fishcakes*, 1998.
Davidson, James, *The Greeks and Greek Love*, 2007.

Davidson, Michael, *The World, The Flesh and Myself.*
Davis, John Paul, *The Gothic King, Henry III*, 2013.
Dover K.J. *Greek Homosexuality*, 1978.
Duby, George, *William Marshal*, 1985.
Eisler, Benita, *BYRON*, 2000.
Erlanger, Philippe, *Buckingham*, 1951.
Erlanger, Philippe, *The King's Minion*, 1901.
Everitt Anthony, *Augustus*, 2006.
Everitt Anthony, *Cicero*, 2001.
Fagles, Robert, *The Iliad*, 1990.
Forellino, Antonio, *Michelangelo*, 2005.
Fraser, Antonia, *The Gunpowder Plot*, 1996.
Frieda, Leonie, *Catherine de Medici*, 2003.
Gayford, Martin, *Michelangelo*, 2013. A beautiful book.
Gillingham, John, *Richard the Lionheart*, 1978.
Goldsworthy Adrian, *Caesar*, 2006.
Goldsworthy Adrian, *The Fall of Carthage*, 2000
Goodman Rob and Soni, *Rome's Last Citizen*, 2012.
Gore-Browne, Robert, *Lord Bothwell*, 1937.
Graham-Dixon, Andrew, *Caravaggio* 2010. Fabulous.
Graham, Robb, *Strangers*, 2003.
Grant Michael, *History of Rome*, 1978.
Grazia, Sebastian de, *Machiavelli in Hell*, 1989.
Guicciardini, *Storie fiorentine*, 1509.
Halperin David *One Hundred Years of Homosexuality.*
Harris Robert, *Imperium*, 2006
Herodotus, *The Histories*, Penguin Classics.
Hesiod and Theognis, Penguin Classics, 1973.
Hibbert Christopher, *The Borgias and Their Enemies.*
Hibbert Christopher, *The Rise and Fall of the Medici.*
Hibbert, Christopher, *Florence, the Biography of a City.*
Hibbert, Chris, *The Rise and Fall of the House of Medici.*

Hicks, Michael, *Richard III*, 2000.
Hine, Daryl, *Puerilities*, 2001.
Hirst, Michael, *The Tudors*, 2007.
Hogan, Steve, *Completely Queer*, 1998.
Holland Tom, *Rubicon*, 2003
Hughes Robert, *Rome*, 2011.
Hughes-Hallett, *Heroes*, 2004.
Hutchinson, Robert, *Elizabeth's Spy Master*, 2006.
Hutchinson, Robert, *House of Treason*, 2009.
Hutchinson, Robert, *Thomas Cromwell*, 2007.
Isherwood, Christopher, *Diaries*, vol. one, 2011.
Jack, Belinda, *Beatrice's Spell*, 2004.
Johnson, Marion, *The Borgias*, 1981.
Jouhandeau, Marcel, *Ecrits secrets*, 1988.
Kanfer, Stefan, *Marlon Brando*, 2008.
Kelly, Ian, *Casanova: Actor Lover Priest Spy*, 2008.
Knecht, Robert, *The French Religious Wars 1562-98*.
Köhler, Joachim, *Zarathustra's Secret*, 1989.
Lacey, Robert, *Henry VIII*, 1972.
Lacy, Robert, *Sir Walter Ralegh*, 1973.
Lambert, Gilles *Caravaggio*, 2007.
Landucci, Luca, *A Florentine Diary*, around 1500.
Lawday, David, *Napoleon's Master*, 2007.
Lev Elizabeth, *The Tigress of Forli*, 2011.
Levy, Buddy, *Conquistador*, 2009.
Lewis, Bernard, *The Assassins*, 1967.
Livy, *Rome and the Mediterranean*
Lubkin, Gregory, *A Renaissance Court*, 1994.
Lyons, Mathew, *The Favourite*, 2011.
Macintyre, Ben, *The Man Who Would Be King*, 2004.
Mallett, Michael and Christine Shaw, *The Italian Wars*.
Manchester, William, *A World Lit Only By Fire*, 1993.
Mancini, *Caravaggio*, circa 1600.

Marchand, Leslie, *Byron*, 1971.
Martin,Brian Joseph, *Napoleonic Friendship*, 2011.
Martines Lauro, *The Plot against the Medici*, 2003.
McLynn, Frank, *Richard and John, Kings of War*, 2007.
McLynn, *Marcus Aurelius*, 2009.
Merrick, Sibalis, *Homosexuality in French History*, 2001.
Meyer, G.J. *The Borgias, The Hidden History*, 2013.
Meyer, G.J. *The Tudors*, 2010.
Miles Richard, *Ancient Worlds*, 2010
Miller, David, *Richard the Lionheart*, 2003.
Mitford, Nancy, *Frederick the Great*, 1970.
Moore Lucy, *Amphibious Thing*, 2000.
Moote, Lloyd, *Louis XIII, The Just*, 1989.
Mortimer, Ian, 1415, *Henry V's Year of Glory*, 2009.
Nelson, Craig, *Thomas Paine*, 2006.
Nicholl, Charles, *The Reckoning*, 2002.
Niven, David, *Bring on the Empty Horses*, 1975.
Noel Gerard, *The Renaissance Popes*, 2006.
Norwich, John Julius, *Absolute Monarchs*, 2011.
Oosterhuis, Harry, *Homosexuality and Male Bonding*.
Ostrow, Steve, *Live at the Continental*, 2007.
Parini, Jay, *Empire of Self, A Life of Gore Vidal*, 2015.
Parker, Derek, *Cellini*, 2003, beautifully written.
Pascal, Jean Claude, *L'Amant du Roi*, 1991.
Pernot, Michel, *Henri III*, Le Roi Décrié, 2013.
Petitfils, Jean-Christian, *Louis XIII*, 2008, wonderful.
Plimpton, George, *Truman Capote*, 1998.
Plutarch's Lives, Modern Library.
Pollard, .J., *Warwick the Kingmaker*, 2007.
Polybius, *The Histories*.
Rader, Dotson, *Blood Dues*, 1974.
Read, Piers Paul, *The Templars*, 1999.

Reston, James, *Warriors of God*, 2001
Ridley, Jasper, *The Tudor Age*, 1998.
Robb, Peter, *The Man Who Became Caravaggio*, 1998.
Robb, Peter, *Street Fight in Naples*, 2010.
Rocco, Antonio, *Alcibiade Enfant à l'Ecole*, 1630.
Rocke, Michael, *Forbidden Friendships*, 1996.
Romans Grecs et Latin, Gallimard, 1958.
Ross, Charles, *Richard III*, 1981.
Rouse, W.H.D., Homer's *The Iliad*, 1938.
Ruggiero, Guido, *The Boundaries of Eros*, 1985.
Sabatini, Rafael, *The Life of Cesare Borgia*, 1920.
Saint Bris, Gonzague, *Henri IV*, 2009.
Saslow, James, *Ganymede in the Renaissance*, 1986.
Schama, Simon, *Citizens* 1989.
Schiff, Stacy, *Cleopatra*, 2010.
Schom, Alam, *Napoleon Bonaparte*, 1997.
Scurr, Ruth, *Fatal Purity*, 2007.
Sellner, Edward, *The Double*, 2013.
Seward, Desmond, *Caravaggio – A Passionate Life*, 1998.
Shapiro, James, *1599*, 2005.
Shaw, Aiden, *Sordid Truths*, 2009.
Simonetta, Marcello, *The Montefeltro Conspiracy*, 2008.
Sipriot, Pierre, *Montherlant sans masque*, 1982.
Skidmore, Chris, *Bosworth*, 1988.
Skidmore, Chris, *Death and the Virgin*, 2010.
Solnon, Jean-Fançois, *Henry III*, 1996.
Spoto, Donald, *The Kindness of Strangers*, 1997.
Stewart, Alan, *The Cradle King, A Life of James VI & I*.
Stirling, Stuart, *Pizarro Conqueror of the Inca*, 2005.
Strathern, Paul, *The Medici*, 2003.
Stuart, Stirling, *Pizarro - Conqueror of the Inca*, 2005.
Suetonius, *The Twelve Caesars*.

Tacitus, *The Annals of Imperial Rome*.
Tacitus, *The Histories*.
Tibullus, *The Elegies of Tibullus*.
Tuchman, Barbara, *A Distant Mirror*, 1978.
Tuchman, Barbara, *The March of Folly*, 1984.
Turner, Ralph, *Eleanor of Aquitaine*, 2009.
Unger Miles, *Magnifico*, 2008.
Unger, Miles, *Machiavelli*, 2008.
Vanderbilt, Arthur, *Best-Kept Boy in the World*, 2014.
Vasari, essential in our understanding of the times.
Vaughan, Richard, *John the Fearless*, 1973.
Vernant, Jean-Pierre, *Mortals and Immortals*, 1991.
Vidal, Gore, *Palimpsest: A Memoir*, 1995.
Violet, Bernard, *Les Mystères Delon*, 2000.
Virgil, *The Aeneid*, Everyman's Library, Knopf, 1907.
Viroli, Maurizio, *Niccolo's Smile*.
Ward-Perkins Bryan, *The Fall of Rome*, 2005
Warren, W.L., *Henry II*, 1973.
Weinberg, Williams and Pryor, *Dual Attraction*, 1994.
Weir, Alison, *Eleanor of Aquitaine*, 1999.
Weir, Alison, *Mary, Queen of Scots*, 2003.
Weir, Alison, *The Princes in the Tower*, 1992.
Marvelous.
Weir, Alison, *The Wars of the Roses*, 1995.
Wheaton James, *Spartacus*, 2011.
Whyte, Kenneth, *The Uncrowned King*, 2008.
Williams Craig A. *Roman Homosexuality*, 2010.
Williams John, *Augustus*, 1972.
Wilson, Derek, *The Uncrowned Kings of England*, 2005.
Winecoff, Charles, *Anthony Perkins, split image*, 1996.
Woods, Gregory, *Homintern*, 2016.
Wotherspoon, *Who's Who in Gay and Lesbian History*.
Wright, Ed, *History's Greatest Scandals*, 2006.

Wroe, Ann, *Perkin, A Story of Deception*, 2003. Fabulous

Zachks, Richard, *History Laid Bare*, 1994.

INDEX

Please note that the page numbers are *passim*. An example, Cesare Borgia 76 – 102 means that Cesare Borgia is found within these pages, but not necessarily on *every* page.

Lightning Source UK Ltd.
Milton Keynes UK
UKHW021855190520
363537UK00015B/192